Poetry Ireland Review 114

Eagarthóir/Editor

Vona Groarke

© Poetry Ireland Ltd 2014

Poetry Ireland Ltd/Éigse Éireann Teo gratefully acknowledges the assistance of The Arts Council/An Chomhairle Ealaíon and The Arts Council of Northern Ireland.

LOTTERY FUNDED

Poetry Ireland invites individuals and commercial organisations to become Friends of Poetry Ireland. For more details please contact:

Poetry Ireland Friends Scheme, Poetry Ireland, 32 Kildare St, Dublin 2, Ireland

or telephone +353 1 6789815; e-mail management@poetryireland.ie

FRIENDS:
Joan and Joe McBreen, Desmond Windle, Neville Keery,
Noel and Anne Monahan, Ruth Webster, Maurice Earls,
Mary Shine Thompson, Seán Coyle, Andrew Caldicott,
Henry and Deirdre Comerford

Poetry Ireland Review is published three times a year by Poetry Ireland Ltd. The Editor enjoys complete autonomy in the choice of material published. The contents of this publication should not be taken to reflect either the views or the policy of the publishers.

ISBN: 1-902121-53-8   ISSN: 0332-2998

ASSISTANT EDITOR: Paul Lenehan (typesetting, proofreading, pre-publication)
with the assistance of Claire Brankin
IRISH-LANGUAGE CONSULTANT: Aifric Mac Aodha

COVER IMAGE: *Tronie* (2013), oil on canvas, by **Cian McLoughlin**
DESIGN: Alastair Keady (**www.hexhibit.com**)

Printed in Ireland by **Brunswick Press Ltd**, Unit B2, Bluebell Industrial Estate, D13

Contents

Poetry Ireland Review 114

Editorial

December. The year homes in on itself, tilts towards a nub of darkness before the tilt back in favour of light. This is factual and literal: it accounts for itself in science and experience. It is a known truth made visible through the roofbox of Newgrange on 21 December. On the shortest day of the year there, if the weather is kind, the inner chamber of the tumulus is lit by a beam advancing up the passageway, honing itself to a tip of light against the furthest wall. It gilds stone and shoes and dust in the air. It is factual and literal, yes; but though we may admire its scientific bravura, I doubt if astronomy or maths are why Newgrange matters so much to us.

I think we love Newgrange because we love metaphor, the slip and purchase of it, the way it tells its truth slantwise, as Emily Dickinson, (that master of imagistic shock-tactics), advised. Metaphor is an act of negotiation, at its most effective when it is between an abstract entity and verifiable fact; between, you might say, a rock and a hard place; or, in the case of Newgrange, between two hundred thousand tons of rock and soil, and one beam of light. 'There is no real knowing apart from metaphor', according to Herr Nietzsche, and though I'm loathe to inflict him on you at this time of year, you can see he's got a point.

I wouldn't dream of pinning that beam of light to a fixed point of meaning. That would ruin the metaphor, the way it suggests and insinuates, its resonance and play. Its meaning is intuited rather than declared, and this subtlety gets closer to a usable truth than most so-called facts ever do. We know it, of course we do, and we know it not on the tongue or in the cerebellum, necessarily, but in the place Mr Yeats once called 'the deep heart's core'.

Funny to think that poetry – where language works the hardest and is most sincerely put to the test – is also the place where language slips out of its self-tied ties. But this is exactly the kind of play metaphor makes, between what is known and what is not; between visual detail and abstract idea; between the word in all its physical presence, (its set and shape, the sound it makes), and the un-word, the white page surrounding the words; a poem's negative space, the containing, encompassing silence into which languages edges incrementally in order to make visible, to see.

Newgrange deploys not a single word to make its one, lit point, and yet seems close to poetry, to how a good poem works. In mystery, in certainty; in silence and in words: it is all a rummaging for some kind of truth that cannot, despite itself, be pinned down to a matter of fact.

Here, though, is a matter of fact: one interview, one essay, twenty-eight recent books reviewed, forty-five new poems. Numbers and words. And something else. Something unpindownable. Like light.

– Vona Groarke

Adam White

POSTCARDS FROM GREENLAND

1.

JAKOBSHAVN GLACIER

Today I saw the big one, defreezing
tongue of the ice sheet, blue alps calving
and collapsing into the ocean.
Its thaw water weeps.

A welling outlet that draws a crowd
north of the Arctic Circle, and draws
the two miles-thick rug of ice out from under.
They say the land is depressed by the weight of it.

Three quarters of a berg weighs down on your mind.
The bigger ones lump in the fjord
until melt lets off the handbrake
for their earth-quaking grating on the earth.

2.

DAMAGE CONTROL

On the lam, Erik the Red risks his neck
reporting back
with the lie of the land he's found out west, how
it's greener. Leaving again, long boats in tow,
his exiled heart's a little breezier;
missing home now will be that much easier.

Daragh Breen

ALICE MAHER, THROUGH THE LOOKING-GLASS

February's looking-glass moon is low
and makes a paper screen of our bedroom window
and every time a car passes down the lane
its headlights drag the hedge's silhouettes
across the back of the curtains,

widow's ivy regurgitated from the throat
of a toad-licker in a battered wooden shed,
up to her oxters in a gin-bath
and her hair that won't stop growing
snow-deep all over the floor.

They say that she has a retinue of trained otters
at her beck and call, that sleep in the
lake of her hair all winter long,
and every summer they burn willow for charcoal
so that she can continue to render their world.

Peggie Gallagher

DAY'S END

Sometimes it is simple;
a quiet street, weathered stone and brick,
air so fine it could trick the senses
through which six decades have slipped
like beads through a child's fingers –
the convent rookery and the light
that bleeds through.
All as we left it, and still here,
trailing our suitcase home.

Martin Burke

BEYOND

Essay the river and essay the docks, the dock-workers
The goods of merchants stocked in containers
The cranes, the lifts, the pulley wires and ropes
Say something about this, place it in a time-frame
Decry what's lost but love what remains
See the river continue beyond the bend you cannot see beyond.

Michelle O'Sullivan

FURLED

deep creased
neither my scars
nor yours are fresh
and though we are
mid-point
our old erosions
can lay defeated

while this furled
word of love
takes its time
to become again
open
linen the turned bed
of our hearts

Michelle O'Sullivan

PARTIAL

Waking, not to you
but the wind shaking summer
through the trees, pink shadows
gold through the greens.

And these blackbirds, dissatisfied
looking for fruit, fleck
and dip their dew-wet beaks –
yet there is no sad singing.

One curtain is pulled aside,
the other is still drawn.
For the time being,
this is the light we're living by.

Michelle O'Sullivan

QUARRY

A loosening of leaves, mineral-golds thin
to brown and make temporary footnotes
around the trees.

This soft chime of rustle and tick, open windows
rafting cool air, a white morning sun
clean as a hare's bone.

Last night the sky turned stars, paper-lanterns
lifted from a ridge of cobblestones,
and a luminous cable shaped a bear.

There was the wind too; dim sounds came
from the back of the house, like mouth
breathing down a bottle's neck.

Had I been quieter, I might have heard
the tree-talk of oaks or a lark skitter to its attic –
wood noises from the far-off woods.

Maybe it was no loss, the maze
of sound I thought I'd missed,
my ear held at a wilderness.

Eamon Grennan

OF NATURE, GOD AND MAN

Seán Lysaght, *Carnival Masks* (The Gallery Press, 2014), €11.95.
Kathryn Maris, *God Loves You* (Seren Books, 2013), £8.99.
George Szirtes, *Bad Machine* (Bloodaxe Books, 2013), £9.95.

In *Carnival Masks*, Seán Lysaght's sixth collection, the emphasis once
again is on poems the poet, with tact and his own brand of understated
eloquence, draws from his observations of the natural world. As always,
what I'm most impressed by in his work is the way he finds a language
for the exact vibrations of his sympathetic response to what he finds
there. Without sentimentality he manages to give the sheer, animated,
ordinary yet mysterious presence of that other world its due. Always,
too, in a Lysaght poem, the natural facts carry with them some depth
charge that connects with the human world – in its emotional, even its
political being. Such poems are never merely descriptive – though he has
a marvellous keen eye and sharp ear for shape, texture, colour, sound. In
essence they are *meditations*, expressing that area in himself where
thinking and feeling coalesce into a persuasively personal language of
response, quietly dramatising a deeply held, persistently reiterated
philosophy of being-in-the-world.

Consider, for example, a poem like 'Hare' with its characteristic
touches of descriptive exactitude and emotional intensity: the hare
'burdened with too much lore / [...] finds a gap in the hedge / and is off
for months, years, / across rushy hillsides and the outback of whins'.
Landscape and creature, at home with each other, sketched in a few deft
strokes. But Lysaght is never content with sketch. He pursues his quarry,
the hare, folding it into human society and the sport of coursing:

> He spurns the law's release
> to fling himself at derelict townlands,
> recovers his form in long grass
>
> where the air shines with cables
> of abseiling spiders ...

There's a fine variety in this collection – with relaxed love poems,
including 'Jessica and the Butterfly' ('a set of marbled wings / give[s] its
signal, open and shut'), and a brief heartbreaking elegy ('In Memory Of
My Father'), partly in Irish, for his father, from whom it seems the poet
drew his passionate attachment to the minutiae of nature:

And there I stood again
at a brilliant wall of gorse
looking for a way through,
with birds all calling for you, of course.

In addition, as well as some translations, there's a sonnet sequence that wrestles with that vexing figure, Edmund Spenser, as well as a large number of poems set in an Italian landscape, far from Mayo. Although colourful and evocative of their foreign environment, these last seem less immediately striking than those rooted in the Irish context, and less in possession of an always palpable if unspoken underground of darker emotional implication. But taken as a whole, *Carnival Masks* – in the way it pushes at the boundaries of Lysaght's quietly self-possessed poetic world, shows a poet writing himself into the full maturity of his craft and scrupulous art.

Spry, worldly-wise, formally light of foot and touch, an easy adept of rhythm and rhyme, humorous with a sometimes dark edge or core, the best poems in London-based American Kathryn Maris's second book, *God Loves You*, possess velocity of utterance, sly shifts of tone, spoken immediacy, and a sharp-eyed comic-satiric buoyancy that carries off each poem with no fuss and no leftover. This is especially true in the first section (of three). These poems seem the most natural product of Maris's art, poems in which her angled tilt on and understanding of the world seem unstrained, at energetic ease with themselves. Many of them feel like full-voiced addresses from a gently torqued version of self to variously inflected versions of 'the world out there': for example, 'Darling, Would You Please Pick up those Books?' (a cracking sestina), 'Will You Be My Friend, Kate Moss?', and 'I Imagine We Will Be Neighbours in Hell'. It's the *address* aspect here, preserving the essentially spoken quality of the language, that works so well, and is the register where Maris seems most at home, as in the Kate Moss poem: 'We have so many things / in common, like you're pretty much my age; / we share initials; the circumference of / our thighs is basically the same (I checked).'

As the title of the collection (and of the second section) lets us know, God is a preoccupation in many of these poems. In fact God or a version of 'Him' lurks behind a lot of what's here, and while the poet's response (or 'belief') can be lighthearted, nonetheless (the poems imply) she also takes Him seriously. 'Why' is an example of the mixed mode – playful, yet with serious intent. Again the sense of the spoken drives the poem colloquially forward:

Before I was God
as you know Him to be

> I liked to sit
> on my quark bench
> and stretch my legs,
> take in the void,
> have a snooze
> then wake and sketch
> plans for the future.

A little distance from Genesis, yes, but the whimsy has its serious point. In the poems that work best, I love this unsettled poise the poet manages to maintain, the mix of tones that makes us active participants in the poem, not quite knowing how to respond to its serious yet strange little inner drama.

The second section also has a number of prose poems. For me these are less successful, their more calculated (sometimes *faux* biblical) rhetoric too mannered and too willed to work either in silent reading or for a live audience. Mention of a live audience makes me think that the best of Maris's work must go down with real serio-comic force in public readings, while some poems that seem on the page merely clever may still succeed through the live presence of the performing poet. But pieces like 'Angel with Book' – which rises to a fine colloquialising of Rilkean afflatus – or 'Street Sweeper' – with its lovely, apposite phrase, 'God's slovenly generosity' – these work, whether in silence or in spoken form. There is an honest generosity in this second collection, its poems the expression of an imagination and a sensibility alive in and to the world, and – while seeing into its dark corners – still able to remain cheerful, steady, and creatively unafraid.

Bad Machine is George Szirtes's (by rough estimate) twelfth collection. Its 111 pages contain poems of such impressive variety and achievement that the reader (this reviewer anyway) can only stand back, take a deep admiring breath, and point to qualities that especially take his or her fancy. Richly textured with an array of expertly wielded forms, Szirtes convinces one that in his skilful hands the art itself is nature – even within the dizzying, hypnotic confines of villanelle, acrostic, sestina, or *canzone*.

Szirtes's poetic speech mixes the formal and the demotic, but always remains, lovingly, speech. His work is dipped in the brine of history, the salt of politics, the tart honey of lyricism. His voice is – as James Wright remarked of his own ambition – that of the grown man: at home in and at odds with the world he must willingly inhabit.

The 'bad machine' is the body, and the book (with a nod to *Hamlet*?) is shaded by an abiding sense of mortal threat, human vulnerability. But the condition, in poem after poem, is wonderfully resisted by the sheer energies of expression, form, art – energies that don't overcome the common enemy, but resist and won't succumb to it either. And over all this, there's Szirtes's recognition of the paradox at the heart of things:

> Terror of death. Desire for it. Nothing new
> in the options *either* / *or*. No need to dread
> the grim reaper, or to worry about the new
> morning that won't be there waiting.
>
> [...]
>
> So there's the balance that we know is just.
>   – 'CANZONE: TERROR OF, DESIRE FOR'

The poems are full of questions – questions enough to conjure a world, a world in which this philosopher poet, for whom the language itself is instrument of probe and discovery, must go on seeking and saying and again seeking, saying. The poems carry many literary echoes: Auden, Rilke, Roethke, Larkin among others. But Szirtes absorbs influences and makes his own of them. The echo, faint or clear, is in its own way, nourishment – the poet's own healthy nutrition source.

In the midst of this volume's riches, there are a few poems that don't have the same specific charge as the great many that do. Some seem to turn only on their own cleverness, or into little puzzle-plays in the manner of R D Laing (e.g., 'Say So'), or extend into the underweighted, as with 'McGuffin's Tune'. And I wish his editors had put dividing title marks between the discrete sections in the text, as in the list of contents, since each section is a small unit in itself, and it'd be better to make this clear to the engrossed reader. Quibbles. No matter – there's more than enough to fill more than a single volume here, all gathered into this single plenteous, robust, exhilarating collection.

John Fitzgerald

1 WTC

A schoolyard in Tribeca, mid-morning, mid-winter,
brittle sunshine, sharp inland wind, the yard
ringing with swarming cries that gather like gulls
around a tall black figure in a dark leather jacket
consenting with a kind smile to take each coloured rubber
football and punch it with the top of his big clenched
piston fist up high up into the air up where the
grinning children's faces follow their eyes rising beyond
fist, beyond head, beyond steel school roof to their own each small
ball reaching its exhilarating but dependable point of fall,
and indifferent to the still continuing unreal upward going
of the vast glimmering glass backdrop to it all; this one thing
that will one day become for some of them their everything
that is impossible and beyond reasonable reach, like
the first unexpected sight of the rest of their lives.

Jason Irwin

MAIN STREET

From the front porch we guessed
colours of cars, drank lemonade
out of paper cups and listened
to the Kapinski kids get beat
by their mother. That dissonance
reverberated through back yards
where Virgin Marys kept vigil
in bathtub grottoes, and old man Tilly,
senile and drunk, promised
to pulverise us for throwing rocks
at his truck. Twenty years now

since he surrendered
to the Elks Memorial Home and the Kapinskis
moved to some God-forsaken
Des Moines, or South Dayton,
after their mother's fourth husband
realised he was a woman, trapped
in the wrong movie, I think of them,
wonder what became of Priscilla,
who showed me her privates
behind the rabbit cage when we were nine,
or Timmy and George, who were all teeth,
sandy hair and bruises

no one ever questioned, not even
Miss Butler, who taught third grade.
I remember Sally, too,
blue as the swimming pool where they found her,
too young to cross the street alone
or read *Hamlet*. Sometimes I drive
by the old house on Main Street,
I can still see them:
faces and fists against glass.

George Vulturescu

THE ANGEL AT THE WINDOW
  – for my son, Cosmin-Leonard

The house with windows shut
in my village Tireac

How is it that from so great a distance I still can see
through its window
the carollers passing along the road?

Fool, in childhood you stood
in the window and waited to see the angels
passing along the road

Now the angel is at the window and looks through me
as along the road I gather loose horseshoes
lost by the prince's silver stallion.

            – translated from Romanian by Adam J Sorkin and Olimpia Iacob

Asa Boxer

OLD ART DECO WALK-UP

The stairwell door is a misfit,
leaning roughly in a tilted frame.

A precarious kiss of brass tongue
and brass lip barely holds

these two together. And still
you must jiggle, spin and jostle

an absurdly loose knob to tease
the tongue back in, and again

to release it and close the door.
There's no way in or out

without this fuss. Always the door
and his mate stammering,

being either rattled in union,
or tricked apart with a clamour.

So steep is the staircase, it is
nearly a ladder. It seems a trial

meant for the penitent alone.
But as soon as you're involved

with this edifice, you come under
her influence: the crooked, creaking,

teetering funhouse feeling of being
in a place just lateral to the norm.

You can expect the lock at the top
of the stairs is not a one-handed

flick-of-the-wrist affair and won't yield
before you've questioned your sanity.

Inside, the plumbing calls for mending,
as not even the faucets can get it together

to have warmth on tap: it's either scalding
or cold. And the old iron rads coiled

under the windows draw the air
through their ribs with the vapour

of all your breath and sweat,
wringing you dry to the particle.

Andrew Fitzsimons

THE PATTERN HISTORY WEAVES

John Montague, *New Collected Poems* (The Gallery Press, 2012), €25.

John Montague is one of the leading figures of the generation of Irish
writers who came to prominence in the 1950s; his achievement is large
and his position within Irish poetry after mid-century secure. One of the
things his *New Collected Poems* does, apart from reminding us of his
significance, is offer the chance to measure how far we have come since
the drear days of the Ireland of Montague's literary beginnings. Not very
far, you'd have to say:

> And there, on a ravaged hillock
> overlooking the road,
> the raw inheritor of this place,
> an unfinished hall.
> — 'ROSELAND'

These are lines that could have been written this week. Montague's
descriptions of 1960s and 1970s Ireland have become timely again, and
remind us that there was another time, in the not too distant past, when
economic rampage was visited upon us, and by us. What comes across
most vividly in these pages is his abiding concern with remembering the
lives of people roughed up by visible and invisible hands, by history and
by economics:

> Like shards
> Of a lost culture, the slopes
> Are strewn with cabins, deserted
> In my lifetime. Here the older
> People sheltered, the Blind Nialls,
> Big Ellen, who had been a Fair-
> Day prostitute. The bushes cramp
> To the evening wind as I reach
> The road's end. Jamie MacCrystal
> Lived in the final cottage,
> A trim grove of mountain ash
> Soughing protection round his walls
> And bright painted gate. The thatch
> Has slumped in, white dust of nettles

On the flags. Only the shed remains
In use for calves, although the fuchsia
Bleeds by the wall, and someone has
Propped a yellow cartwheel
Against the door.
                    – 'THE ROAD'S END'

Montague is at his best when details are allowed speak for themselves: the white dust of nettles, that fuchsia bleeding by the wall, the yellow cartwheel against the door; but here, as at times throughout the writing, there is a tendency to the grand statement and over-explanation ('Like shards / of a lost culture'). This over-explaining also mars some fine early poems ('My uncle played the fiddle – more elegantly the violin').

In the nearly twenty years since his first *Collected Poems* (1995), co-published by Wake Forest University Press and The Gallery Press, Montague has continued to publish and this *New Collected Poems* extends that book with revisions and additional poems and by including the three collections which have emerged since then, *Smashing the Piano* (1999), *Drunken Sailor* (2004) and *Speech Lessons* (2011). As with the earlier book, rather than proceed chronologically through Montague's career, *New Collected Poems* places the three major 'orchestrations' first: *The Rough Field* (1972), *The Great Cloak* (1978), *The Dead Kingdom* (1984), as if to acknowledge where Montague's real achievement lies. It is hard to argue any differently. These books introduced to Irish poetry an anthropological intensity and breadth, in their examination of Ulster's past and present; the indefatigable nature of love; and the lingering hold on the imagination of personal places. Some of the lyrics from *Poisoned Lands* (1961), though, represent his finest work: the portrait of the emigrant in 'Murphy in Manchester', and the proto-Heaney of 'The Water Carrier':

You stood until the bucket brimmed,
Inhaling the musty smell of unpicked berries,
That heavy greenness fostered by water.

The editorial quandaries surrounding Philip Larkin's *Collected Poems* come to mind: the arrangement plays up the deliberated coherence of individual volumes (though it should be noted that there have been slight changes of title and order) at the expense of giving a picture of chronological poetic development. The arrangement does, however, give proper prominence to Montague's extraordinary personal story: born in Brooklyn, returned as fosterling to Co Tyrone, separated from mother and brothers, to be raised by his father's sisters in Garvaghey, the 'rough field' of his most well-known book:

So I found myself shipped back
to his home, in an older country,
transported to a previous century,
where his sisters restored me,
natural love flowering around me.
       – 'A FLOWERING ABSENCE'

That 'return' to a place he had never previously visited intensified the eye
and ear of the youngster, and issued in a poetry concerned with rites and
rituals, of country life most especially, and also a preoccupation with
speech, founded in the casual brutality of a childhood classroom and a
harridan of a schoolmistress:

'So this is our brightest infant?
Where did he get that outlandish accent?
What do you expect, with no parents,
sent back from some American slum:
none of you are to speak like him!'

Stammer, impediment, stutter:
she had found my lode of shame,
and soon I could no longer utter
those magical words I had begun
to love, to dolphin delight in.

And not for two stumbling decades
would I manage to speak straight again.
Grounded for the second time
my tongue became a rusted hinge
until the sweet oils of poetry

eased it and grace flooded in.
       – 'A FLOWERING ABSENCE'

I quote at length because there is a lot of what lessens Montague here:
the masked self-regard ('our brightest infant'), the mushiness ('magical
words', 'dolphin delight'), the inconsistent and awkward rhymes and
half-rhymes; and yet, for all that, the poem delivers tremendous emotional
power. The most moving poems tackle the hard stuff of his childhood,
and his fractured relationship with his parents. His mother, that 'fertile
source of guilt and pain', is remote and unloving, and yet:

I never knew, until you were gone,
that always around your neck

> you wore an oval locket
> with an old picture in it,
> of a child in Brooklyn.
>   – 'THE LOCKET'

When Montague sticks to the unvarnished matter of fact the rewards are great, and would that more of the work stuck to the *ars poetica* formulated in 'A Bright Day': 'a slow exactness / / Which recreates experience / By ritualizing its details' (*A Chosen Light*, 1967). Many of the early poems affect the Auden-meets-Movement manner prevalent in the 1950s and early 1960s, as well as the concern with social diagnosis the manner demanded, and a little goes a very long way:

> Evening brings the huntsman home,
> Blood of pheasants in a bag:
> Beside a turf-rick the cackling peasant
> Cleanses his ancient weapon with a rag.
>
> The fox, evicted from the thicket,
> Evades with grace the snuffling hounds:
> But a transplanted bailiff, in a feudal paradise,
> Patrols for God His private grounds.
>   – 'WILD SPORTS OF THE WEST'

But the book shows how brave Montague could be: *The Great Cloak* chances versions of Jaccottet, Apollinaire, poems from the Irish ('Liadan Laments Cuirithir'), and poems spoken from the female perspective in its evocation of sex, marriage, infidelity, and love. The Ireland of sexual frustration and sexual violence is here too. In 'The Wild Dog Rose' an old woman, inevitably a *cailleach* to the younger Montague, but to the adult 'a human being / merely, hurt by event', after a life spent alone, one night in her own home suffers a brutal attack from a drunken neighbour, 'crazed / with loneliness'.

Montague's concern with people and the places that have made and unmade them, has given us wonderful poems of social portraiture ('Like Dolmens Round My Childhood', 'Witness', 'Clear the Way'), but also a tendency toward the gossipy and sociable, and a concern with himself as poet within a social world of artists. There is a lessening of poetic energy in the later volumes, and the gossipy, garrulous side to Montague is given too much its own way. But there are still some wonderful poems. In 'Still Life, with Aunt Brigid', we see all the many strengths of the work, in the gentle empathy of the evocation of a loved one, and a past:

> ... as, crossing the cobbles at night
> on some last errand (are the hens
> locked in safely, the calves foddered,
> the yard gate looped closed?)
> the swaying light of the storm lamp
> or a hand-sheltered candle, flickers
> around her frail figure, limned in gold
> and shadows, like a Rembrandt.

That 'yard looped closed' enlivens the mind enough to see the unmentioned rope and then there are the wonderful specifics of the 'swaying light' and the 'hand-sheltered candle', and the chiaroscuro of 'limned in gold / and shadows', but after all this work, was there really any need to tell us the scene is 'like a Rembrandt'? Ultimately, though, what this poem shows is the gift of tenderness, a feeling for other people's lives that has been there from the first in Montague's writing, and remains there at the end.

The book is as handsome as we have come to expect from The Gallery Press (a minor blemish: in the notes Gandhi's name is misspelled; and, though some of its poems remain, *Forms of Exile*, his first book, has been excised from the list of contents), with a striking image by Patrick Scott on the cover. Personally, though, I prefer the textual layout of that original *Collected Poems*, particularly with regard to *The Rough Field*, where the orchestration of poem and prose benefited from an almost dramatic deployment of text upon the page, with smaller font size, more play with indentation and a larger amount of white space. The juxtaposition of texts is diminished here, no more so than in the 'A Collage of Religious Misunderstandings' of 'The Bread God' section of the sequence. I miss also the useful introduction to *The Rough Field* of that earlier *Collected*, which provided biographical and poetic context, setting the poem's rural Ulster material alongside the 'open form' mode adapted from American examples: Williams, Olson, Duncan, and the more 'rooted' MacDiarmid of *A Drunk Man Looks at the Thistle*. The poem's strengths are many. Montague has a gift for anatomizing his society, and in this work his descriptive excesses and weakness for romantic cliché (the 'silent dalliance of youth') are kept in check by anger, by the compelling facts of his own story and 'the pattern history weaves / From one small backward place'.

Robert Wrigley

EXPERIMENT

I went into the winter woods
on the coldest night of the year,
spread a moth-eaten wool blanket
and undressed and lay there

for as long as I could bear
with nothing on, and rolled over
once and stayed far longer
than I should, until I could

almost not re-enter my clothes
for shaking, and could not
tie my bootlaces and almost
lost my left boot in the snow

on the way back to the cabin,
no more than a hundred yards away
but I almost missed it
and walked around it twice

before finding the door
and falling through, and
crawling to where the stove
popped and the shimmer of heat

from its surface was invisible
in the shudder and liquidity
of my sight, and I lay there
believing as I had hoped I would

that I had made it as far
and as close and as deep and as high
as I could have, and slept then,
waking later poached in sweat,

and slithered without rising
out of my clothes again,
and watched, from between hearthstones
a tussock moth – weeks or months frozen

in the nook it had taken shelter in –
twitch, then jerk, then flutter,
and with great difficulty flip itself
onto its feet, from which it flew

into the warm open air of the cabin,
over the holey blanket
and among the five candles still burning
of the eight I'd lit before I left.

Gavan Duffy

VIEWER

Who could love these winter mornings
all murky edges and limping clock?
The fuzzy frost and foggy houses,
our mountains convinced
they can't be seen.

I saw letters while I lay half asleep,
written cleanly and spaced slightly apart,
like pieces from a puzzle laid out
for consideration, or the bits
of something valuable shattered
in a fall.

Downstairs is the hardworking fire,
the tea mug with no handle
steaming like a chimney on your desk;
the nimble lips and rattling lies,
shadows like bruises on the floor.

We could talk for a while about the usual things,
hungry thoughts, your favourite sadness
and the urge to start again. I could go
quiet then and let you sing to yourself in a whisper,
as you sometimes do. Until your eyes clear.
Until you remember your foul mood.

I lie back and close my eyes instead.
The letters form a signature now,
like two tiny queues.
The initials are large and potbellied,
and holding the others back.

Sarah Sala

TANAGER STREET

Home after dark
I listen for the electric
pierce of the television,
for her slipper shuffle.

I wait to hear the tumble
of clothes in the dryer,
the kettle whistle
from the stove.

Not even a vacuum
disturbs the silence;
I am late and want
to be forgiven.

Christopher Mulrooney

FOE

it's an ancient quarrel he says what's mine is yours
he means it rest assured as he has nothing well
there is the point of argument let's ask him then
no argument really says he what's mine is yours and indeed
he seems most richly endowed with cities farms factories and
    nohow deprived
on second look what a blink that must have been so what's he
    complaining about
what's mine is yours says he a real thoroughgoing bastard that

Joey Connolly

STRUGGLE AND RISK

Andrew Fitzsimons, *What the Sky Arranges* (Isobar Press, 2013), £10.
Marianne Burton, *She Inserts the Key* (Seren Books, 2013), £8.99.
Caoilinn Hughes, *Gathering Evidence* (Carcanet Press, 2014), £9.95.

There will always be a question as to how poetry in translation should
situate itself between two hard-to-reconcile tasks. Should a new volume
of translations strive to educate us about the poetic culture, tradition,
and tropes of the original language, or should it work to bring across the
book's ideas and feelings into our culture, tradition, and poetry? The
question is particularly pronounced when facing literary cultures hugely
different from our own. This is true of the culture which shaped (and
was shaped by) the *Tsurezuregusa* of Kenkō, from which Fitzsimons has
derived these poems. It's hard to know, for us, the formal games played by
medieval Japanese Buddhistic essays / prose fragments in a stream of
consciousness (very loosely: more properly *zuihitsu*, 'follow the brush').
Luckily, Fitzsimons has provided us with several clues for answering the
question of which literary culture we're interested in with this book.
Principally, by simmering down 243 'essays' to 30 short poems, and by
adopting recognisably English metrics and occasionally rhyme.
     'The Risen Tide' is one such poem, with its loose tetrameter, its
borrowings from Latin, and its conclusive rhyme – it ends, 'What does
day teach the day? / The peach and damson trees / in the garden will not
say.' It is interested in asserting itself as an *English* poem (English-
language: some commentators have found here a statement about Irish
politics, although this seems to me a little forced), and yet those last lines
turn a hard shoulder to any attempt to extract what we might conceive
of as revelation. We are being told that we will be told nothing, but in
such a way that we're brought back to those damson and peach trees,
explicitly stripped of their symbolic or allusive functions. Peaches as
peaches, damsons as damsons: they may know what the day teaches the
day, but they're not for telling. The plump full rhyme only reinforces the
feeling of self-containedness, of quiddity. But if Fitzsimons has lost what
Linda Chance has in mind when she writes, of the original text's subject,
that 'the most correct perception is a blend of the provisional and the
empty', he has perhaps found a sense of a mysterious, withheld fullness
which flowers in the tradition of English-language modernism.
     Consequently, those of Fitzsimons's poems which seem to find a
modern subject – complaining about the 'neophytes' of new technology,
or the blindness to tradition of local government – are much less successful.

Erin Quinn originally from Canada, now permanently resident in Ireland

Adam (from the series 'Breaking Point'), 2013
Photograph, archival pigment on fine art paper, 128 x 90 cm

Shortlisted, Hennessy Portrait Prize 2014

Hugh O'Conor, from Dublin

Beckah, Dublin Airport, 2013
Photograph (film, B&W 120) on liquid acrylic, 101.6 x 101.6 cm

Photo © Hugh O'Conor
Shortlisted, Hennessy Portrait Prize 2014

Geraldine O'Neill, from Dublin

Is feidir le cat Schrödinger an dá thrá a fhreastal, 2014
Oil on canvas, 200 x 210 cm

Photo © National Gallery of Ireland
Shortlisted, Hennessy Portrait Prize 2014

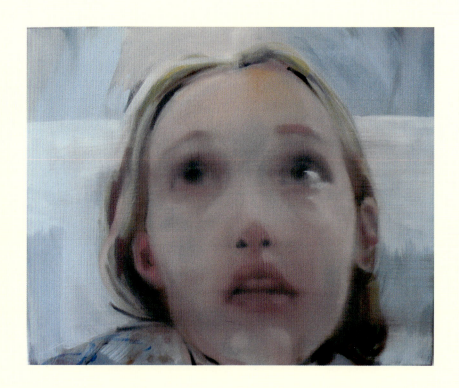

Helen O'Sullivan-Tyrrell, from Bray, Co Wicklow

The Convalescent, 2014
Oil on canvas, 40 x 50 cm

Shortlisted, Hennessy Portrait Prize 2014

Although they engage in the familiar project of renovating old or classical authors (think of Hughes's *Tales from Ovid*, Mahon's Sextus Propertius, or Nagra's recent *Ramayana*) into something less fusty and austere, they simultaneously lose the valuable sense of a meditative profundity – summoning adroitly our idea of Japanese wisdom – which he elsewhere crafts so successfully.

One of the most interesting things about Marianne Burton's *She Inserts the Key* is that its two best poems are two of the most technically flawed of the collection. This is true of 'The Emperor and the Nightingale', and also 'Sparrowhawk', which describes a couple observing that bird as it gets caught on a thorn-bush and remains for a few seconds an 'exhibit' with its 'barred feathers pinned wide for our inspection', before it frees itself and gets away. The poem ends:

> leaving us piecing together what we'd seen
> with what we would claim later we had seen.

The grammatical repetition (with its subtle alteration) – along with the way the last line moderates 'piecing together' to suggest the two accounts will always tessellate somehow – speaks intriguingly about the project of this kind of observational, anecdotal poetry: we are, after all, getting right now only what Burton is claiming to have seen. The content of the poem is thrown into doubt, and we're left with only the language in which to find our truth.

But the really interesting thing is that this poem remains so interesting despite its flaws. It is besieged by problems of vantage, slipping into free-indirect narration to describe the hawk's prey as 'lunch', even though the poem is predicated on describing the act of witness. Then we get the hawk's 'eyes extruding, beak gaping', although the scene is ostensibly witnessed from behind the bird. Perhaps this is excusable as depicting precisely those subtle revisions made in any recounting of a story in which the poem is interested; certain weak terms, jarring repetitions and metrical petering-out are not. The point, though, is that using 'protruding' and 'extruding' in the same line, or picking weak and incongruous verbs (the hawk 'lay crucified' after it 'slammed' into the thorn-bush), seems not enough to bring down the poem's valuable piece of thinking.

In fact, throughout most of Burton's collection, the poems avoid entirely such mistakes, and yet fail to rise above the flat and dully conventional. Burton is clearly a competent poet in at least two ways, and it would be short-sighted to assign the shortcomings of *She Inserts the Key* to her lack of talent. The truth is that this book has no flaws except what flaws are possessed by the work of mainstream contemporary British poets. It is no less chimingly musical than Duffy's *The Bees*, no less charmingly quirky than Copus's *The World's Two Smallest Humans*, no less chummy or eager-to-please than Armitage's *Walking Home*. It is no less original than Gwyneth Lewis, no less complex than Christopher Reid. It is no less subtle or ambitious or thoughtful than a raft of recent collections shortlisted for major prizes. Unfortunate for a doubtlessly dutiful, attendant, and competent Marianne Burton, then, that so much of this type of literature fails, fundamentally, to say very much.

In *Gathering Evidence*, Caoilinn Hughes is more interested in expanding outwards towards new areas of research – as her title suggests – than sitting back on convention and consensus. And as well as having the ambition, Hughes has the ability and the willingness to take risks, and the combination leads to a very striking first collection.

The particular risk Hughes encounters most frequently occurs when her several bejargoned idioms come into tension: although these poems borrow most heavily from the vocabulary of science, there are also religious, romantic, lyrical, and political dictions here. The risk, then, is that the elements of some of these languages come to seem decorative or gratuitous; Hughes has to find a way of holding them in a relationship – house-of-cards like – so that none of them collapse into merely decorative metaphors for something else. The opener, 'Avalanche', is representative: 'When the avalanche came down on us // it did not come down on us in a holy light', works against 'Was it fluid dynamics, glaciology / or meteorology you surveyed?'; and, later on, 'I should never have collapsed in love with a physicist'. The avalanche in question functions variously as a poetic opportunity for a rich description of an actual avalanche; as a metaphor for the overwhelming onrush of love; as a demonstration of the physical basis of incredible phenomena; and, through Hughes's denials, as the uncomfortable intrusion of religious implication into catastrophic events. The wonderful thing, though, is that these various threads aren't kept apart. Each is allowed to make comment on the others: the collapse into love is illustrative of the physics of an avalanche just as much as the description of being buried in snow illuminates the various isolations of being in love.

There are several poems that work in this way in *Gathering Evidence*, and they all feel like an engaging struggle: can Hughes pull it off this time? Occasionally, as in 'Rational Dress', she can't, and the subject matter – Marie Curie's social as well as scientific iconoclasm – sufficiently overwhelms the poetry that the radiant multivalency which Hughes achieves elsewhere isn't possible. Other poems again, like 'King of the Castle', fight almost audibly throughout to rein in their scientific subject matter to a more poetic mode of communication. These poems, as struggle and risk, range from bemusing to exhilarating, but the presiding feeling is that Hughes has produced something genuinely original.

James Conor Patterson

THE POSTCARD

'... caught so pitiful and tattered and beyond retrieving –
like a child's paper kite snagged on a utility wire.'
— James Allen, *Without Sanctuary: Lynching Photography in America*

In an act of violence rendered delicate
by the dime-store postcard, what you're witnessing
isn't really a death at all. Laura Nelson
is levitating. The slack-mouthed rabble
reflected below her are bobbing away
like catfish. Some grasp frantically and take
up the slack about her shattered neck
until it heals again. Some of these are children.
A light goes on in her death-coiled eye,
the trees are sepia-grey – though really, green –
and once the rope has loosened a bit
she notes the wind that blows the other way.
Her stabs are closed like lips. Someone hands
across her infant daughter and three men repair
her bloodied gingham with invisible stitches.
They climb outside her. Their come is spirited
away. And now all that's left are the backward
gibes, the dust died down on the road,
a tow sack draped across her head and shoulders
and too many words unpacked from this bottomless trunk.

John McKernan

I KEPT TOUCHING

The driver's licence
With my picture

The Social Security
With only numbers
And my name

I put a sheet of music
Up to my ear
Looked out
At the silent stars

Walked to the room next door
That man was still breathing
His eyelids would not stop blinking
I could smell his terror
Huge   High as the ceiling

Justin Quinn

CONVERSATION GALANTE

She says the dead come back for a mere flake, fleck
or fume of favourite food. A fragrant air
we hardly know is more than they can bear.
For them the speed of our bored talk is breakneck.

She says when we lean in to catch the scent
that rain showers summon from the April earth
dead millions groove themselves into the berth
of our one sense. They are engulfed, content.

He says let them do what they want, these dumb
sad hordes of shades. Do you think that they'll come
the moment I push back the floral hem

of the summer dress you look so lovely in,
and lift it off, leaving you just a grin?
What do you reckon that will do to them?

Justin Quinn

LONG BRIDGE

Long because the floods
spread out at this turn –
different coloured muds,

crackling rushes, fits
and flights of water, a
long-awaited blitz,

sweeping briskly stray
plastic, ordure, crime-scene
tape and tyres away.

Half a concrete mile
spanning to the west.
I gaze north a while.

Two halves of the land
are held in place by it.
But from where I stand

the other bank can't even
be made out; the fog makes
it hard to believe in.

There are longings crossed
by other longings. Mid-
way over, feeling lost,

I hear the current thrum
against the concrete piers,
whispering, urging: come.

Justin Quinn

EMBASSY DINNER

A square of twilit lawn seen through French doors.
The affable minister murmurs to the host.
Summer evening. Aperitifs. A roast.
Breezes glide across the parquet floors.

The waiters move in silence. Now the wives
draw dutifully together for a talk
of family and schools, and watch the clock.
Two years to go till our first child arrives.

We live five floors up in a block of flats
across the city. Half a mile of muck
to walk through from the Metro. Like diplomats,

we say, 'No, after you,' and fall in bed,
still laughing, stripping off to fuck.
Nothing of those hours has touched us yet.

Daisy Fried

TAKE THREE

Paul Muldoon, *The Word on the Street* (Faber and Faber, 2013), £12.99 hb.
Sinéad Morrissey, *Parallax* (Carcanet Press, 2013), £9.95.
Eavan Boland, *New Selected Poems* (Carcanet Press, 2013), £12.95.

Should we treat a book of rock song lyrics from Paul Muldoon, one of
the best contemporary poets, as a mere lark? More than that: after all,
Sappho, the mother of us all, sang her poems, the very first girl with a
guitar (or in her case, lyre), singing about love. The lyrics in *The Word on
the Street* aren't all or even mostly about love, but they are about
contemporary life, and – since song is the basis for poetry – should be
taken as seriously as they're meant, as part of the great pre-print
tradition, of song and breath, and heart. (Go to Muldoon's band's
website to hear the music: **http://waysideshrines.org**).
  'It may be too late to learn ancient Greek', begins 'It's Never Too Late
For Rock 'n' Roll':

> It may be too late to dance like Fred Astaire
> Or Michael Jackson come to that.

The nifty thing about this song is that it ultimately rejects the pathetic
aging rocker anthem for gentle wit and realism. The words belie the title:
'It may be too late to think that you're / Never too late for rock 'n' roll.'
But, the lyric ends: 'We have to believe we have to believe / We can lose
those last twenty pounds.' The defiantly middle-aged goofiness charms.
  In songs as in poems, Muldoon's fascinated with vernacular expression,
with tweaking cliché:

> It's the party line
> The official position
> Everything's still fine
> At Seventeenth and Mission
> It's all still sweet
> It's all hunky-dory
>
> [...]
>
> The word on the street
> Is we're done.
> — 'THE WORD ON THE STREET'

Muldoon's songs (again like his poems) are studded with proper names, money troubles, current events, celebrities. 'Azerbaijan' is in millennial spirit, a hybrid of Cole Porter's suave wit and Bruce Springsteen's crumbling industrial-state yearning:

> I worked for years
> In oil and gas
> Our engineers
> Once flew first-class
> But the factory's
> run out of steam ...

These are songs well worth reading.

Sinéad Morrissey is by temperament discursive. Her longer poems take journeys; discursive pressure is also brought interestingly to bear on shorter poems. *Parallax*, which won last year's T S Eliot Prize, is full of precision meanders. Three-page 'A Matter of Life and Death' begins, 'On the afternoon I'm going into labour so haltingly it's still easy / to bend and breathe', then digresses to World War II television, the Labour party, David Niven, and Technicolor. In fifteen-line 'Shostakovich', the Soviet composer remembers sounds of his youth, mostly wind 'moaning through the stove', in wheat husks. And:

> In all my praise and plainsong I wrote down
> the sound of a man's boots from behind the mountain.

Domestic experience is Morrissey's constant throughout *Parallax*, showing up in the diary-like, Dorothy Wordsworth-inspired '1801', as well as in a number of apparently autobiographical maternal poems. But Morrissey displays range in subject as well as in style. There's a poem about Soviet-era farming, an ekphrastic poem about a Hans Holbein painting, and the creepily fascinating 'Blog': 'I don't have girlfriends but I do have sex / with a different woman about three times a month', writes the blogger.

> ... There's this tiny electrical thrill
> gets passed like an egg-yolk slipping
> between the cups of its own split-shell.

American readers sometimes find that writers in English across the Atlantic play it close to the vest, dwelling modestly in the quotidian instead of signposting their epiphanies. I suppose we Americans like a loud-mouth fuss, which leads us to our own poetic crimes and

misdemeanours. Morrissey's got a deep sort of quiet and every-dayness.
But there's fuss too. It's restrained. You've got to listen for it.

Eavan Boland's *New Selected Poems* debuts seven new poems, including
'Re-reading Oliver Goldsmith's "Deserted Village" in a Changed Ireland',
wherein Boland mimics, in theme but not form, Goldsmith's
condemnation in heroic couplets of rural depopulation and the pursuit
of wealth. Its message is uncomplicated; its music a pleasure:

> Here in our village of Dundrum
> The Manor Laundry was once the Corn Mill.
> The laundry was shut and became a bowling alley.
> The main street held the Petty Sessions and Dispensary.

Boland's good eye and ear moves with economy from event to opinion.
In bulk, she can seem relentlessly reverent. But this takes place around
sudden spikes of emotion, such as this move from appreciation to
emasculation, first published in *The Journey and Other Poems* (Arlen House,
1986 / Carcanet Press, 1987):

> The chimneys have been swept.
> The gardens have their winter cut.
> The shrubs are prinked, the hedges gelded.
>   – 'SUBURBAN WOMAN: A DETAIL'

Robert Frost spoke of 'sentence tones that haven't been brought to book
… real cave things'. Boland sometimes squanders her cave things,
allowing the performance of resentment to devolve into petty complaint.
'An Irish Childhood in England, 1950' (*The Journey*) begins with a wonder-
fully snitty portrait of alienation:

> The bickering of vowels on the buses,
> the clicking thumbs and the big hips of
> the navy-skirted ticket collectors with
> their crooked seams brought it home to me:
> Exile …

But the poem concludes with a teacher chiding the Irish child for a
mistake of the vernacular: 'you're not in Ireland now'. Is complaining of
other people's sins enough – whatever true oppression is behind the sin –
to conclude a poem begun in a finer place?

But Boland's direct address and smoulder is often thrilling. In
womanly things, she sees grace and constriction: 'I wonder about you',
begins 'The Rooms of Other Woman Poets' (*Outside History*, 1990):

... whether you think, as I do, that wild flowers
dried and fired on the ironstone rim of

the saucer underneath your cup, are a sign of
a savage, old calligraphy: you will not have it.

'Writing in a Time of Violence' (*In a Time of Violence*, 1994), with its
historical sweep from Ireland to America and back and its understanding
of individual experience within that, is a major poem. No forced
reverence here. Just fearful force:

...we are stepping into where we never

imagine words such as hate
and territory and the like – unbanished still
as they always would be – wait
and are waiting under
beautiful speech. To strike.

Matthew Sweeney

THE DREAM HOUSE

The dream house was yellow
and had no chimneys. Its one
window was round, a porthole
so big a child could stand in it.
The door was smaller, and red,
with a golden chain and padlock.

Around the house was a Zen
garden of sand raked in circles,
with occasional bonsai palmtrees,
each with its own yellow spider
swaying on its gossamer web.

Behind the house was a long,
flat mountain that sloped left.
White goats could be seen on it,
and a few climbers, or walkers –
the gradient being so gentle.

Inside the house was a circular
staircase with yellow mosaics
leading to the inner, upper haven.
There was no furniture downstairs.
There was no one living there.

Matthew Sweeney

The Beauty Institute was closed
so I went to the harbour, where
boys in blue were trying to toss
boys in red into the water, with
the aid of wooden lances, while
Arab music tootled along. I myself

was lacking in instruction, so I sat
in a bar on the Corniche with a beer,
composing a curse for the editor
who'd dropped me. I forced myself
to encompass this in a sestina,
a form I knew he hated, but as

a wet blueboy was fished out of
the churning water, I found my
sestina being derailed by beauty,
the concept of it. What was it?
These boys in their coloured hoops?
Their girlfriends clapping them?

Brassens' echoes on the waters?
Monet's water lilies in Giverny?
A poodle dancing on the table
in *Chez Jacques*, where the grilled
squid goes well with a carafe of *Picpoul*?
A bald baby crawling under it?

It was too much, too big a subject.
I tore the page out of the notebook,
scrunched it into a ball and chucked
it into the water, then headed up
the high road to a view of the sea,
and the soothing *Cimetière Marin*.

Mary Noonan

The artist is sitting, perfectly still,
by his mulberry tree, watching
it. He has been in that pose all day.

The white moths have flown
through my open window,
drawn by the light of a bedside lamp.

They are everywhere – cloaking
the walls, sleeping in the folds of sheets,
crawling over the shoes on the floor.

I try to flatten some with newspaper
but they are too many, and I lie down
among them. Soon, they cover me,

their anaemic wings lining the creases
of my eyelids, lashes thrumming
to the sound of a thousand tiny wings

flicking. In the bed, I rustle. Moths are
spinning from hairs, slinking over the skin
of my scalp and pubis. I lie in a rictus.

In the morning, I walk on a flittered
bridal veil of wings, from bed to bathroom.
I pass the artist. He is sitting

by the fish tank, watching his black
piranha slip through cool water,
behind glass. Has he been there all night?

Stephen Sexton

THE DEATH OF HORSES

The death of horses haunts the horses,
sours gallons of parochial milk,
and rots the berries on the cane.
The bones of horses keep arranged

largely in their living shape. A rib
or thighbone missing here, carrion
clumped around a hoof as though death
was elsewhere overthrown: a skeleton

growing back its flesh – the pastern,
gaskin, stifle, loin. Those horses
left to fly-graze a hillock
of granite, weed, and ankle-break

have died a death of intervals.
The mind boggles, that is to say
the mind is full of ghosts which is
to say the mind haunts itself,

its own black mane, its obsidian.
Iron chimes at intervals on
the stone as coronets fester
and one by one the shoes drop off.

Iron echoes piecemeal across
the valley, its memory strides
home past maggots in the ditch,
through some farmer's skelfing floorboards,

up through his son's shivering bones
whom he tries again to coax to sleep.
The river curses TV static.
It's too dark and not dark enough.

Padraig Regan

TRACKS

'It was something he had written.'
   –Yasunari Kawabata

At first the snow was a distraction in a what-strange-weather, small-
   talk kind of way,
but by lunchtime Belfast was smooth and gleaming white as an egg.
   It was a Friday.
In just a few hours the streets had grown a fleece six inches thick.
   My shoes were ruined
and the moisture was doing its slow capillary creep up the backs of
   my trouser legs.

And all this in March! I could have sat all day by that café window,
   so relieved
to be indoors and distracted by the music hall dumb-show of
   wobbly pedestrians desperate
to keep their feet on the pavement which only yesterday had
   seemed so dependable,
that the weather reports falling like commas between songs on the
   radio

and the menu's description of 'Mediterranean' salad drifted into the
   book
I was only half reading so the sentence formed: *When he arrived in*
   County Antrim,
Oki went directly to the Miyako Hotel. He asked for green olives and feta
   cheese.
The book, by the way, was Kawabata which is dangerous at the best
   of times

but when combined with snow proved way too much for my
   personal barometry,
and left me with a need to trawl through auction sites for Edo
   period ceramics
and wonder how those cows that I passed on the drive home, flick-
   ering across the windows
like scratches on a strip of film, would compare to the stoic cows of
   Hokkaido.

We knew that things were serious when the radio gave out advice
    not just for motorists
but on the care of animals and the elderly; it told us to abandon all
    unnecessary
journeys, to look into our hearts and stock the cupboards of our
    frail neighbours –
the weatherman was revelling in his own voice; he had never had
    such airtime.

Those yards between the car and the front door were a trek through
    the Toyama prefecture.
Inside the radiators were gurgling their way to full power and Oki
    was listening
to a chorus of temple bells weaving and unweaving over the rooftops
    of Kyoto,
although privately he might admit that they sounded better on the
    radio,

that the feeble *kotatsu* and cups and cups of sake were doing nothing
    to distract him
from the cold. The chapter caused fragments of my own New Years
    to sift into the March
evening: rosé wine, dance music, the warm nap of a navy blue duffel
    coat.
And walking along the Lisburn Road under the sodium glow of
    streetlamps for so long,

and so slowly I almost thought our destination was a pretence (I
    was wrong,
we had simply missed the turn off). It was just cold enough for a
    sparkling frost to bloom
on the tarmac and I was trying to explain the significance of striking
    the temple bell
108 times to greet the New Year but I was shivering, slurring my
    words,

and the streets were punctuated with the shouts of people popping
    out of their own stories
for a smoke. I turned on a lamp sometime during the festival of the
    full moon as Otoko
and Keiko were watching the darkness gather in their garden and
    discussing revenge on Oki.
My window was clouding up with snow like a rush of static on an
    old cathode-ray.

I always imagine that Vermeer's *Girl Reading a Letter at an Open
    Window* is overlooking
a street where the cobblestones have been swallowed by a shelf of
    out-of-shot
snow. In that sense, I'm just like Brueghel, who after finding his
    USP in winter landscapes
laid a blanket of lead-tin white over any unsold scenes lying around
    his studio.

One more example: when I drafted a poem about the bells of Kyoto,
    which was really
about all the things I wish I could have said that New Year's Eve, I
    added snow –
to be honest I transplanted some lines into this. *When Oki was tired
    of writing,*
or when a novel was going badly, he would lie down on the couch. Me, I
    write about snow;

I gather some sibilant phrases, look up white in the thesaurus and
    string it all together
with an absent 'you'. Perhaps it all goes back to that night when
    Belfast was so cold
it could have been mistaken for a town on the Sea of Japan and we
    were lying
on the stiff grass, our breath condensing on the air in puffs as thick
    as rabbits' tails –

only the beauty of it had been heightened – my head was on his shoulder
listening to the flutter and pulse beneath, and then somehow (or
    maybe it was later)
we were standing very close together, kissing even, and I could feel
    his hand,
his amazingly warm hand on the flesh of my back like some sleeping
    animal.

Outside the sky continued to unfurl big, blustery sheets of snow.
    Across the province
trains were stalled and street signs placed under erasure. Saturday
    was cancelled;
what else was there to do but sit wrapped in blankets and watch
    farmers on the BBC News
digging blue-lipped, frost-tarnished sheep out of drifts like a crop of
    damaged marrows?

Philip Coleman

'THE STRANGE IMPERFECT MASONRY OF POETS'

Macdara Woods, *Collected Poems* (Dedalus Press, 2012), €16.99.
Harry Clifton, *The Holding Centre: Selected Poems 1974-2004* (Bloodaxe Books, 2014), £12.
Gabriel Fitzmaurice, *A Middle-aged Orpheus Looks Back at His Life: New and Selected Poems* (Liberties Press, 2013), €11.99.

It's hard to imagine a poet walking into a bank and presenting a poem as proof of identity. Whether such a thing ever happened to Macdara Woods or not, his *Collected Poems* confirms his place as a major Irish poet and shows, throughout its more than 400 pages, that he has been passionately committed to the art of poetry for nearly six decades. The story about the poet in the bank is told in his poem 'West Going West', from *Artichoke Wine* (2006), where Woods also recalls stopping into a shop 'for bread and milk in Carrigahoult' and being asked:

> *You're a writer then –*
> *you write yourself?*
> I'm quizzed by the man in the shop
> *Do you know James Liddy?*
> *Or Brendan Kennelly?*

Doubtless Woods knew Liddy, and probably knows Kennelly, but the question is less interesting for any literal truth it might yield than for the way that it circles back on the issue of what it means to be a poet and what might be at stake in declaring oneself to be one. Throughout his work, Woods returns again and again to this question of what it means to be a poet. 'How then could I compose a poem – / I cannot yet compose myself', he wrote in 'The Dark Between the Days', collected in a section gathering work written between 1966 and 1972, while in another early poem called 'Rockpools' (written between 1973 and 1986) he describes the way that:

> The pen in my hand encumbers
> both instinct and thought
> confuses for a moment craft and numbers
> and the white page – wilful as wind
> remains the landscape of the albatross
> mountainous blank unmarked

The encumbrance of the pen here can be read as an interesting response to Seamus Heaney's image of the poet taking up his pen to 'dig with it' in his well-known poem 'Digging'. Like Heaney, indeed, Woods sees the 'craft' of writing as an activity that involves much more than the mere enumeration of line and syllable. In short, both poets appreciate what Patrick Kavanagh called 'the secret sign that's known / To the artists who have known the true gods of sound and stone / And word and tint'.

'West Going West' concludes with lines that further affirm Macdara Woods's commitment to this belief in 'the secret sign' as Kavanagh understood it. His image, of the poet *surviving / the same crooked passing of time / and the strange imperfect Masonry of poets*', points on the one hand to the physical activity of making poems as a mason works with stone, but the word 'Masonry' also suggests involvement in a system of 'secret signs and passwords' (*OED* 3.b). A belief in the mystery of these signs allows Woods to have a vision of Kavanagh in Umbria (in the poem of that title, written in 2004) but it is hard won. '*Keep it up for twenty years the poetry*', Woods recalls Kavanagh telling him in Leland Bardwell's front room at 33 Leeson Street in 'Leland: PS from Yalta'. His *Collected Poems* charts a journey through many dark periods where Woods's faith in himself and his art wavered – there are poems of great candour about alcoholism here, for example, from 'The Dark Sobrietee' and 'Serial Flashback' to 'Here in the Darkness' – but throughout all of his work there is a consistent intensity of vision, a desire to discover 'how / the world / unfolds – this search for sense // And shape'. Sometimes – as in the sequence from which these lines are taken, *In the Ranelagh Gardens, September 2002* – Woods produces poems of great musical power and the text of *In the Ranelagh Gardens*, indeed, was set to music by the composer Benjamin Dwyer and performed in Dublin in 2006. Like Kavanagh, Woods has a great ear for music and the poem simply entitled 'Song' from his latest collection, *The Cotard Dimension* (2011), shows this. He is also an acute and uncompromising observer of social life, however, and the *Collected Poems* contains many political poems that should be counted among the most significant poetic contributions to public discourse written by an Irish poet over the last forty years. 'Lazarus in Fade Street, Summer 1986' provides an incisive critique of a particular historical moment – a note tells the reader that it 'was written in the contentious atmosphere of the 1986 Divorce Referendum' – while 'Driving to Charleston', written in 2004, reflects on the global cultural and moral impact of the USA's invasion of Iraq the previous year.

Writing about Stephen Crane in 1950, John Berryman concluded that 'his eyes remained wide open on his world'. Recollecting times spent living, working and travelling abroad in places ranging from London to Marrakesh, Umbria to St Petersburg, Macdara Woods's *Collected Poems* affirms a similar sense of worldly alertness and engagement, but he is also a wonderful poet of fatherhood and familial connection. The many references to his son Niall and his wife, the poet Eiléan Ní Chuilleanáin, together with verse letters of one kind or another to friends and companions down the years, make this volume a kind of autobiography-in-verse, but it is one in which the reader is constantly surprised by the intensity of Woods's poetic vision, his desire to shape words across lines in ways that reflect his pursuit of sense. He embraces a principle of metrical and stanzaic open-endedness that allows him to range freely between closed and open forms, but at all times, and no matter what subjects concern him, Woods's work gives voice and shape to a self for whom there is 'no choice' but to 'carry on' as he puts it in 'Tavernelle Di Panicale':

> *Christ* that I could disentangle
> just one dimension before the day comes back
> working like that Gaelic bard in the womb of the boat
> putting the bones of his poem in place ...

This poem speaks on one level to the frustration of writing – 'hammering at the same blank pages' – but the conclusion it moves towards, like the movement of the *Collected Poems* in itself over the long decades of its composition, summarises the profound generosity of insight that informs Macdara Woods's poetry from the very beginning: 'Niall plays in the sunny yard below / I bequeath him summer and these sunflowers'. There is a darkness about Woods's poems that has its source in many different experiences of frustration and disaffection, personal and political, but his *Collected Poems* allows his achievement to be seen in a clear light – the light of its own humane unfolding.

Like Macdara Woods, Harry Clifton is a poet whose work has always had an international outlook. 'Memory revolves / on a still centre, towards which I move', he writes in 'Michael Praetorius', first published in *Comparative Lives* (1982), but the 'infinite circle' of Clifton's inheritance includes figures such as 'Lanczos the Jew, a ghost out of Hungary / Bartered from Eichmann's ovens / In Forty-three'. This interest in European history, and especially in the legacy of the Holocaust, continues throughout Clifton's work, and the final poem in *The Holding Centre: Selected Poems 1974-2004* – a magisterial elegy for the Romanian-French poet and philosopher Benjamin Fondane, who was murdered by the Nazis in Auschwitz in 1944 – creates a sense of continuity that also gives his poems decisive ethical heft. At the same time, Clifton is not interested in moralising or straightforward condemnation, and his poems often give voice to a troubling sense of disorientation and loss through the experience of being 'caught between war and war' as he puts it in 'Benjamin Fondane Departs for the East':

> I forgive us all, for we know not who we are –
> Irrational, fleeting, caught between war and war,
>
> Faking our own death, in umpteen nation-states,
>   As the monies collapse
> And the borders, and we all transmigrate
> Like souls, through the neutral space on the map.

Although some of his more recent poems – such as those gathered in the collections *The Winter Sleep of Captain Lemass* (2012) and *Portobello Sonnets* (2014) – seem to be more rooted in specifically Irish locales, especially in Dublin and Antrim – Clifton's work is characterised by a feeling of dislocation that arises out of his decidedly European poetic identity and identifications.

Against the sense of uprootedness that pervades Clifton's poems, his work's formal precision and exactitude provides certain refuge. This, perhaps, is the true 'holding centre' of his work, even if the space explored in the title poem of this volume of selected poems ('The Holding Centre') is fraught with 'contradictions / Collapsing upon themselves / Like history'. Based on a visit to the Cambodian border refugee camp at Mairut in Thailand, in 1981, 'The Holding Centre' is a poem that reflects the horrific realities of war ('destitutes crowding in, from the violence // Of the jungle trails'), but it also affirms, however precariously, the desire to live and to love:

> In stateless space
> That frees us, somewhere between
> The absolute kingdoms of justice and of grace
> Where a birdsong intervenes.

Clifton's 'Holding Centre' alludes on one level to W B Yeats's 'The Second Coming', in which the earlier poet wrote that 'Things fall apart; the centre cannot hold; / Mere anarchy is loosed upon the world'. Like Yeats, Clifton's poems hold fast to a central belief in the artifice of poetry even when the surrounding world appears to be on the verge of collapse. This may explain the adherence to formal patterning that characterises Clifton's poems, but there are also moments when 'birdsong intervenes' and the reader becomes aware of a space beyond the confines of poem, page or book, such as that signalled in 'The River':

When I was angry, I went to the river –
New water on old stones, the patience of pools.
Let the will find its own pace
Said a voice inside me
I was learning to believe,

And the rest will take care of itself.

Reading through the poems of *The Holding Centre*, it is clear that Clifton
has taken great care to create a body of work that aspires to the condition
of the 'fissured belltower' he describes in the poem 'In Earthquake
Country'. Recording events of great historical turmoil and loss, for
individuals and communities across Asia and Europe, Clifton's poems
nonetheless tend towards moments of intimacy where, despite 'the
razzmatazz / In a sonic void [...] each of us is alone' ('To the Korean
Composer Song-On Cho').

Fintan O'Toole has suggested that Harry Clifton's *Secular Eden: Paris
Notebooks 1994-2004* (2007) 'is arguably the first great work of Irish poetic
post-modernism', but that claim makes no sense when one considers
either the actual contours of Irish poetic history in the twentieth- and
twenty-first centuries or Clifton's poetic methods. The survival of the
self when confronted with the wreckage of modernity is Clifton's
recurring subject and his poems seek to recover meaning while most
postmodern art proactively attempts to dismantle and explode it.

While O'Toole is wrong about Clifton, however, his description of
Gabriel Fitzmaurice as 'a traditionalist' seems more accurate. Fitzmaurice
is (according to O'Toole) traditional like a 'great singer [using] an old bal-
lad, to train and direct his own unique voice'. However, beyond the
mimicry of certain formal templates – he is particularly fond of the
Shakespearean rhyme scheme (*ababcdcdefefgg*), though his ten-syllable
lines are slack approximations of iambic pentameter – his voice is
'unique' only insofar as his sonnets are by him, he made them. In terms
of their relation to the broader field of contemporary poetry in Ireland
or anywhere else, and the art's longer history – which includes the
history of the sonnet form – Fitzmaurice's poems do not make much of
a contribution. Having said that, his poems of marriage, parenthood,
community and faith – which have been recommended by John McAuliffe
and others – must surely have their audience and to them *A Middle-aged
Orpheus Looks Back at His Life* will provide comfort and amusement. As
Fitzmaurice puts it in the volume's title poem: 'All I wanted when I began /
Was to strike up my guitar and do my thing.' Author of more than fifty
books including numerous works for children, in English and in Irish, as
well as anthologies, collections of essays, and translations, Fitzmaurice's

'thing' is actually far greater than this volume of new and selected sonnets suggests. As he puts it in the closing lines of his brilliant translation of Michael Hartnett's *An Phurgóid*:

This is Ireland, and I'm myself.
I preach the gospel of non-assent.
Love and art is the work I want
as empty as a dipper's nest,
whiter than a goose's breast –
the poet's road with no milestone on it,
a road with no wayside stop upon it,
a road of insignificant herbs
welling quietly from every hedge.

Tom Duddy

STREETSCAPE

If you cannot face the crowded streets today,
cross here and go straight down west bleak street
(through which a dishevelling wind will rush you,
even on a halcyon day), bear left

into high yellow-brick-walled old mill street
where pieces of carton will shift and scurry
after the night before; then take a right –
yes, second right – into old canal bank street

where the chained, locked, tar-painted doorways
figure darkly, even on summer afternoons;
and a short cut at last, bending low, into
the whirling steel-toothed dust of old gaol street.

By the time you reach The Square, you will be
watery-eyed and disconcerted, but
you will have met no one who had to stop
and talk to you in earnest after the horror

of catching your eye, no one from the old country
who had to greet you with surprise and joy,
no one from more recent times who had to
take tender hold of your arm for long enough

to cry: *We must meet up again one day.*
Do give us a call. We're in the book.
Find a bench, then, and sit, good and thoughtless,
until you need to go back the crowded way.

John MacKenna

TENNYSON'S STAR

A lane of falling leaves,
the sun just gone
and air so still the leaves drop straight.

I recognise the wisdom in my father's words:
A steady progress in all things
and if it takes until tomorrow so be it.

Day will break,
bringing the light to finish what's begun.
For now, I'm in these falling leaves.

Martin Malone

INKLING

I got airborne late for these times:
at twenty-one on a freebie to Lourdes,
the town where a mother prayed
for my existence. As the plane eased
its butter-knife through the thick pat
of cloud, I remember thinking about
Shakespeare, Dickens, Donne and Hardy.
How they lived their whole lives not seeing
this, except in some flight of fancy.

Likewise my mother, prayer answered,
could not but stow her baggage
in the overhead locker of the brain,
while she tried to conjure the same
cloudy image I see now. You turn
an already familiar face toward
the ultrasound's pen, re-drawing
yourself as fishbone, heartbeat,
the opening sequence from *Doctor Who*.

An extra-terrestrial hand goes to mouth
while the other mimics your mother
and lays across your chest. Already,
your tongue is working away at her,
or are they the words I shall teach you?
Do you have any idea?

Martin Malone

LUNG JAZZ

Rocking you in *Costa*
      I see it start to riff;
vowels mainly,
in that scat style of a six-month.

      Improvised as Chet Baker,
soloed like Coltrane,
you try them on for size,
      eyes narrowed, mouth freestyle
lost in your self-jazz.

Consonants are to be wary of,
      not trusted
or finished;
      set aside for later.

Take up the buggy's push-and-pull,
count out   a pause,
and discover
the wild love of your own two hands.

Fionn, keep the beat
      and, in your own good time,
tell me what I have lost.

Iggy McGovern

CITY AND GARDEN

Brendan Kennelly, *Guff* (Bloodaxe Books, 2013), £9.95.
Rita Kelly, *Further Thoughts in a Garden* (Salmon Poetry, 2013), €12.
Fergus Allen, *New and Selected Poems* (CB Editions, 2013), £8.99.

If you want to really know the capital of Ireland, try the poetry of born-again Dubliner, Brendan Kennelly; for Kennelly walks the streets of Dublin like nobody else, observing its oddities, chatting with strangers and making poems out of the quotidian. More than half a century on from a debut collection, *Guff* finds him in tip-top form, quizzical, argumentative, and, in spite of the pricks, ultimately consoling.

Kennelly's previous alter-egos of Cromwell, Judas and the roguishly punned Ace de Horner now give way to a head-scratching cave-dweller who (according to the back cover) 'is both mouthpiece and mouthed-off, Devil's Advocate and self-critic, everyman and every writer consumed by self-doubt and self-questioning', and who is asking the question: do 'poets write poems or do poems write poets?'

By way of answer, here is a book-length poem or, if you prefer, 199 individual poems, of variable length, from two to fifty-odd lines, laced with a pleasurable tincture of rhyme. To the deadline-driven reviewer, reading much too quickly, it is the shorter poems that carry immediate charge, punchy aphorisms to charm and challenge, as in 'Notes':

> Adventurous rain plays crucifying notes
> on Guff's open nerves.
> Each man gets the Christ
> he deserves.

Guff's concerns will be all too familiar to Kennelly fans – principally, the opposite poles of mankind's inhumanity to mankind, and erotic love. The latter neatly spears the male of the species in 'At this moment':

> 'Irony is a kind of cowardice,' she said
> 'the kind of thing that has no place
> in heaven or in bed.'
>
> Is Guff an ironist, she'd like to know.
> Well, at this moment,
> No.

Nor does Poetry escape the Guffian lash, as in the opening lines of 'Corncrake': 'Once in the heyday of his youth, / Guff reviewed a book. / Now, in the heynight of his age, / he cherishes the mistake.' *Touché*, Brendan, to which your adopted city of Dublin might respond, borrowing from 'His maker to Guff': 'On, on, dear Guff, on, on, old flower'!

The casual purchaser of Rita Kelly's *Further Thoughts in a Garden* might expect to encounter flora in abundance. But the publisher's note explains that the title is a play on Marvell's 'Thoughts in a Garden', his lament for a pre-Fall Paradise. The collection opens with the title poem, which itself begins with a Marvellian octet but then opts for a variety of stanza lengths. The 'garden' here is the John Hewitt Room within the library of the University of Ulster at Coleraine; Kelly uses the titles of Hewitt's personal library to muse with intelligence and respect on that Ulster writer's concerns, the twin P's of Poetry and Protestantism; and tops it off with a floral display from the gardens of 'closed suburban houses'.

Dublin provides an occasional but significant backdrop in this collection. The poem 'Eithne Strong' finds her in Parnell Square, promising to visit the ailing poet at her home in Eaton Terrace, while 'for Paula Meehan' links the same square with Finglas in a moving remembrance of an unnamed loved one. But the city that dominates the collection is New York. 'Marilyn' is an impressive 17-page celebration of the indomitable spirit of a close friend and of a metropolis, both part of the action in a country at the crossroads:

> Woodstock just happened in the excitement,
> despite the terrified parents back at Bedrock,
> becoming yet more terrified in their lovely clothes –
> Wilma & Fred; Betty & Barney – their well-coiffed
> hair, as the reports began to swell with the numbers.

In her extensive bilingual oeuvre Kelly has tackled the big issues of love and loss, as here in poems such as, 'The Mountaineer' and 'Best Wishes in the 21st Century'. The collection closes as it began, in the University of Ulster, but this time in a real garden. In the eponymous 'Guy Wilson Daffodil Garden at the University of Ulster, Coleraine', the too easy 'fluttering' is cancelled out by a teasing husband/ *husbonde* ambiguity. The garden's creation during the worst years of The Troubles troubled many of the radicalized students of that time, but today all stand hopeful on the edge of some Eden.

Fergus Allen has published five previous collections, the first of which appeared in 1993. But Allen is very much the late developer as he was born during the Irish War of Independence – now, reader, do the maths!

In this *New and Selected Poems* (selected by his daughter, Mary) Allen displays the many talents that first brought him to the attention of Faber editor, Christopher Reid. In his Foreword, Reid writes of 'a delight in firm structure and succinct exposition', and draws attention to the brilliant photographic fixing of the poet's cat in 'Other':

> Weighing me up with his incurious eyes –
> The slits of an armoured car would show more interest.

Allen moved to England after graduation from Trinity College, Dublin and went on to became Director of the UK's Hydraulics Research Station; water is a constant presence in his poetry. The addressee in 'To Be Read Before Being Born' is cautioned that there will be no rehearsals:

> There's only moving water, dimpled by turbulence –
> And no clambering out on to the bank
> To think things over, as there is no bank.

The poems journey to foreign parts, armed with a glossary of place-name and denizen – pangolin, abalone, plumbago, dugong – and a healthy respect for nature that borders on fear, as in 'Flies and Nettles':

> Soon the land will again be coated in nettles,
> Stinging the flesh that strokes them, and all the air
> Will vibrate to the incessant humming of the flies.

But it is not all doom and gloom; there's 'That marshmallow kiss' in 'Surprise', 'my pink-cheeked secretary ... Her bosom snug in Botany wool' in 'The Lives of the Cousins', and the selection closes with a folk ballad, 'The Fall', in which The Garden of Eden is re-born as Guinness's Brewery in you-know-where, ending with:

> And now in this world of confusion and error
> Our only salvation and hope is to try
> To threaten and bargain our way into Heaven
> By drinking the heavenly Brewery dry.

Eamon Grennan

Upriver you see water open again its wide hands of dazzle while
    cloud-shadows collage patterns and the world strobes over your eyes
until like a scarlet conclave of cardinals a pot of Bonnard poppies
    peers out of the dark and traps all the light of Paris or *Le Cannet*
to offer its own thanksgiving as ever for what he as ever
    never tells while in Vincent's still life of apples pears lemons
and skyblue grapes the impression isn't stillness but the purest
    kinetic flow in things as if each piece of fruit each grape cluster
were caught by a swirl that sweeps everything in sight into a bristling
    vortex of incipient vanishing so even leaves on the outermost ring
of the spiral keep growing anti-clockwise fainter like the morning
    dews of Andashino or smoke over Toribeyama or that split second
knife-edge light that lets you see the black sequin on the finch's beak
    as the bird pries from the pendant feeder's wire mesh the toothsome
heart of a sunflower seed and is gone in a flash and you find yourself
    looking with heightened attention again at that abandoned feeder
making with its distinct small pendulum-swings against the window
    a persistent ticking sound.

Mandy O'Neill, from Dublin

Cait, 2014
Photographic print, 76.2 x 76.2 cm

Photo © Mandy O'Neill
Shortlisted, Hennessy Portrait Prize 2014

Comhghall Casey, from Omagh, Co Tyrone

Self-portrait, 2013
Oil on canvas, 40 x 30 cm

Photo © National Gallery of Ireland
Shortlisted, Hennessy Portrait Prize 2014

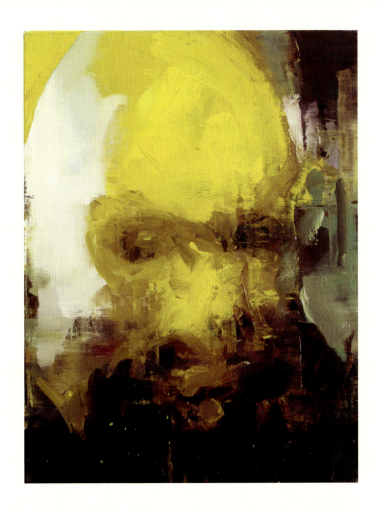

Cian McLoughlin, from Dublin

Tronie, 2013
Oil on canvas, 40.6 x 30.5 cm

John Beattie, from Co Donegal

Still from *An Artist, the Studio and All the Rest ...* (Part 1), 2014
HD colour video with audio

Photo © John Beattie
Shortlisted, Hennessy Portrait Prize 2014

Eamon Grennan

MINUTE

It's how birds are awake to that single minute in the life of the
    world
        that keeps going by that keeps him keeping a peeled eye on
            them in their
infinitely minute changes of colour their speedy heartbeats
    hammering their
        keen little rivets of breath onto air he's staring through at them
            while
Breathe in now says Cézanne as he eyeballs another brilliant square
        inch of the perpetually unsettling here and now gone world *and*
            hold it.

Eamon Grennan

ANOTHER ONE (MARKETPLACE SCENE)

And where are its flowers and birds now its waters cool rooms
  gardens
    or all the haggle-voices flaring from the flagrant bazaar of scarves
      spices
and pomegranates or over the blood-sprinkled iridescent gleamings of
  the fish market
    all lost in the ring of faces leaning over the body of one of their
      own
splayed naked and face down at path-edge where some of the stopped
  onlookers
    hold cell phones high for a better picture of the wire-bound wrist
      the close-
cropped hair the sweat stains on the back of the khaki shirt the stark
  muscular buttocks.

Proinsias Ó Drisceoil

ONLY CONNECT

Edited by Chris Agee, Hugh Cheape, Charles Dillon, Frank Ferguson,
Seán Mac Aindreasa, Murdo Macdonald, Peter Mackay, Aonghas MacLeòid,
Janet McLean, Cathal Ó Searcaigh, Andrew Philip and Frank Sewell,
*The Other Tongues: An Introduction to Writing in Gaelic and Scots in Ulster
and the West of Scotland* (Irish Pages, 2013), €30 / £25 hb.

The Other Tongues is an elegantly-presented anthology of prose and
poetry 'across three jurisdictions (the Republic, Northern Ireland and
Scotland) aimed at bridging the Gaelic and Scots traditions on the two
islands', ranging from the eighteenth-century to the present and drawing
on what it describes as 'the rich interaction between English, Scots and
Scots Gaelic in contemporary Scottish writing'. The absence of 'similar
literary cross-fertilization between Irish and Ulster Scots' is discussed, and
it is an aim of the anthology to create such connections to Scots English
('braid Scots'), the Germanic dialect or language spoken and written
historically in Lowland Scotland and by those of Lowland Scots descent
in Ulster. The book opens with editorial forewords, introductions in
Scottish and Irish Gaelic, translations of same, and an introduction to
literature in Scots English written in standard English. This process takes
thirty pages. Seventy-nine texts follow, most occupying less than a full
page, each accompanied by a visual image and biographical note. These
embrace both poetry and prose, but the brief prose texts often struggle to
achieve the significance demanded of them by the elaborate presentation,
leaving poetry as the dominant element.

The limitation of writing in Irish to Ulster alone means that many
striking connections go unnoticed. Thus, for example, the book includes
poems by the Scottish Gaelic writers Derick Thomson and Iain Crichton
Smith. Both of these have written significant poems on 'clann-nighean
an sgadain', the Hebridean herring women who followed the fleets as
fish cutters. A wonderful poem in Irish, 'Clann iníon na scadán' by Áine
Uí Fhoghlú, published in her 2011 collection *Ar an Imeall* (Coiscéim, 2011),
deals with the women from the Hebridean isle of Barra who did this
same work at Helvick Head, Co Waterford, Uí Fhoghlú's own area.
However the self-imposed geographical limitations of the anthology
necessarily exclude a Waterford text – and a significant contemporary
literary connection. Inevitably the emphasis on Ulster Gaelic means that
Donegal, as the only Ulster county with a living Gaeltacht, is a dominant
source, although Meath's status as an outlying region of Ulster Irish is

acknowledged through the inclusion of an excerpt from the mid-nineteenth-century prose text, *Fealsúnacht Aodha Mhic Dhomhnaill*. Nevertheless, it must be said that the presumption that mutual Scottish-Irish influence on Gaelic literature necessarily followed the lines of geographical proximity is a dubious one given the cultural unity and standardised language of the medieval poetic class which travelled between all parts of both countries indifferently until the collapse of the medieval bardic order.

Literature in Irish has a significant Protestant component, particularly during the nineteenth and twentieth centuries, but the connections this would allow with Presbyterianism in Scotland have somewhat eluded the editors of the present volume. Thus, while an excerpt from the translation by Pàdraig MacPharlàin into Scottish Gaelic of John Bunyan's *The Pilgrim's Progress*, published in 1865, is included, the still-readable translation of the same text into Irish by the Mayo-born Quaker, Earnán de Siúnta ('An Buachaillín Buidhe') published in 1928 and entitled *Turas an Oilithrigh* is not mentioned. Similarly, while an excerpt from the influential nineteenth-century Scottish Gaelic prose writer Norman MacLeod ('Caraid nan Gàidheal') is included, no mention is made of his preaching tour to Ireland in the 1830s or of his (inelegant) attempt to provide texts in Irish of the Scottish Gaelic metrical psalms.

Editorial difficulties abound but a small number of examples will suffice. References to the edited editions on which the published texts draw are not given. The School of Scottish Studies is based at the University of Edinburgh, not the University of Glasgow. The translation of Art Mac Cumhaigh's "Úirchill a' Chreagáin" does not correspond to the verses from the Irish original published in the main text. A particular incongruity is the publication in their original printed form (antique lettering included) of the eighteenth-century Scottish Gaelic texts, notwithstanding the fact that all of these are available in readable modern editions. This, we are told, is intended 'to show how their first readers would have encountered them', but the result is museumisation, particularly as texts in Irish from the same period are presented in readable form as edited by contemporary scholars.

Glasgow English is treated in the anthology as a variety of Scots, which, given that West Central Scots is a component of the dialect, is a sustainable argument. In literary terms it allows Tom Leonard to be included, thus adding to the quality of the Scots component of the anthology, but the superiority of the poetry of Hugh MacDiarmid over all that followed it in the twentieth century revival of Scots poetry is evident in an excerpt published here from *A Drunk Man Looks at the Thistle*. MacDiarmid's admirers in Ireland were likely to share his cultural nationalism, while his influence seems slight among poets in

Ulster of Lowland Scots descent. However, a contemporary Ulster Scots poet – Philip Robinson – may well be worthy of further attention from the uninitiated. The poem selected to represent him is titled 'Oul Licht' and begins:

> Sae dark its lane, tha hoose behin
> A soo's pinke een, in lamp-light blin
> Wairm reek clims up, coultin tae fin
> Afore new licht
> Yin swutch haes lectric's age brocht in
> Wi plestic dicht.

(*lane*: alone; *een*: eyes; *reek*: smoke; *afore*: before; *dicht*: arrayed)

The impression gained of Ulster Scots which, we are told, is 'confined to several rural swathes in north Down and the Ards Peninsula, east Antrim, north-east Derry and the Laggan area of Donegal', is that the vibrancy claimed for it Ireland may be somewhat aspirational, and the fact that the introduction to the Scots poetry has not been written in that language hardly indicates a language in which contemporary issues might be readily discussed.

The Other Tongues as book and object is an artwork in its own right, and relevant editors have been very successful in identifying visual texts which draw out the significance of many wonderful texts, beginning with Séamus Dall Mac Cuarta's 'Fáilte don Éan' and ending with Anna Frater's poem 'Van Gogh'. In spite of its limitations, the book will hopefully aid the appreciation of the long cultural interaction between Ireland and Scotland and all that this bestows by way of future possibility.

Doireann Ní Ghríofa

TAPESTRY

Biddy Jenkinson, *Táinrith* (Coiscéim, 2013), €10.

Biddy Jenkinson is a gifted writer of prose and poetry, yet she doesn't yet enjoy the large readership her work surely deserves. In her oft-quoted 1991 letter to the *Irish University Review*, she outlined her preference 'not to be translated into English in Ireland. It is a small rude gesture to those who think that everything can be harvested and stored without loss in an English-speaking Ireland'. Over twenty years since the publication of this statement, the act of refusing English translation remains as rebellious as it ever was. Jenkinson is a writer of integrity and courage who has never been afraid to turn convention on its head.

Táinrith, her sixth collection of poetry, doesn't disappoint. It takes as its subject the legendary prose epic of the *Táin Bó Cúailgne* (based on the Ulster Cycle tale of a war against Ulster by Queen Medb and her husband Ailill). A revisionary mythopoesis, *Táinrith* engages with its source-material in depth, invoking with dexterity both primary sources and various academic readings of the original text in order to construct something entirely fresh and new.

In her work, Jenkinson has long engaged with the Irish literary tradition in a subversive manner, often giving voice to female characters who have been silenced or subjugated by the original (often male) teller. In this respect, the approach of *Táinrith* should come as no surprise: here, the central aim of the female heroines is to liberate the *Táin* from the dominant patriarchal reading which has suffocated it, and to restore it to its original telling. As with the rest of her body of work, Jenkinson tackles this subject with intellect, wit, and verve, as the reader is brought on a wild and merry jaunt.

To explore the tale, Jenkinson has fashioned a narrative epic poem divided into multiple sections. Epic poetry is a sub-genre that carries the weight of classical tradition – *The Iliad, The Odyssey, The Aeneid, The Divine Comedy* – and has been explored further in contemporary poetry (for example, Alice Notley's *The Descent of Alette*). In terms of locating *Táinrith* within this wider epic tradition, it is perhaps closest to H D's *Helen in Egypt*, which used Euripides's play *Helen* as the starting point for a feminist reinterpretation of the basis of the Trojan War. Although very different in tone and subject matter, these works share common ground in giving voice to a female character on a quest, in an original and challenging manner, and also in raising questions of consciousness, gender, voice, and power. In constructing a modern epic based on an ancient epic, Jenkinson unspools the original, picking up threads and weaving a new tapestry, creating a work alive with vivid detail and contemporary colour. She brings the story of the *Táin* to modern Ireland in a manner which is wholly convincing, and dotted with precisely the right amount of contemporary texture to feel true. She succeeds in transposing this myth into contemporary life in a style more than equal to Anne Carson's verse novel *Autobiography of Red*; Jenkinson's characters in *Táinrith* are similarly nuanced and well-drawn.

Rare though it might be to encounter such a thing in poetry, this is a page-turner. It is difficult to do justice to the pacing with which the plot moves, drawing the reader along through swift shifts from character to character. The degree to which the poetry is driven by the narrative makes it difficult to isolate single quotes, but I've chosen a small selection to illustrate Jenkinson's lush, evocative language:

> D'fhill an oíche an t-ospidéal i bhfallaing oighir.
> Dhein oileán de.

her clever metaphors;

> Tháinig cóta bán amháin eile trín doras
> mar cholúr i ndiaidh na heitilte, agus deifir air.

and her surreal similes;

> féasóg Fhinín, beo mar eireaball sionnaigh ...

In previous collections of poetry, Jenkinson frequently refers to traditional, formally conventional Irish poems and characters with an irreverence, a mischievous glee that is also evident in *Táinrith*. Here she succeeds in communicating both her deep respect and affection for the tradition while simultaneously challenging it light-heartedly. As in so much of her work, she engages with the historical legacy of literature and with the etymological origins of words that we so often accept unquestioningly.

Beneath the intelligence that characterises many of Jenkinson's books, there is a serious sense of subversion. This is by no means a poet to be sidelined or underestimated. To fail to read her work in the language in which it was written is surely to do oneself an injustice. Her writing, whether in prose or in poetry, makes for essential reading.

Seosamh Ó Murchú

GLÓR ANIAR

Cuardaím do ghuth ar bhior na gaoithe
I Márta na bliana nuair is glaise cloch
Nuair is glaine an fuacht a cheaptar
I gcalóga reoite chlog an Domhnaigh.

Cuardaím do ghuth i gciúnas an mhanaigh
A dhéanann allagar leis na failltreacha,
A chuid mianta á seoladh ar an dtoinn
Is an t-am á ríomh i mbriathra molta.

Scaoilim cú na fola dá éill ar iomaire bán,
Á ghríosadh chun do bholadh a chur máguaird
Ar phúir ghalaithe na mbeithíoch méith a chuir
An geimhreadh díobh faoi chomaoin an bhúistéara.

Ní bheireann leis thar n-ais ach a lapa fuilsmeartha
Agus macalla cnagarnach bróg ar imeall lochán seaca.
Béarfad bog orm féin fós go mbeidh síneadh ar an lá
Go gcloisfead arís do gheitgháire ag éalú tríd an arbhar.

Scott Jamison

FIRST DATE

Switch flipped, spring arm pressed against the bell hammer
I am wound and set because he doesn't own a wristwatch.

He is new to this dinner and cinema thing, sets me on the table
as if an alarm clock is the most obvious guest and I want to blush

for us both through my enamel shell. He winds my third arm
knob to ten minutes before ten minutes before the film starts

just to be safe. I know this is a lie – he likes the trailers
dislikes drawn out dinners, hates small talk, doesn't drink

enough to relax, even before the fact that she is b-e-a-u-tiful.
I surprise myself when the trigger hits. Things start like this.

Nick Laird

FUCHSIA

The back lane down to the shore
thinned and greened and deepened
by the seasonal encroachment,
and our mother is there of course,
not dying but walking before us
up the endless blue-roofed corridor,

these hedgerows hung with fuchsia –
that word still flares from itself:
spirant, glide, a suppleness
of opened lips and transfixed fire,
and to you, my sister, each flower
is a little doll dancer, for you too are

coming up, swinging a yellow bucket
crusted with sand, up from the Foxhole
and sunken pillbox to the bungalow.
A fuzzy black caterpillar on a dock leaf
scrunches and unscrunches in the dry heat.
Spires of pink foxgloves. Insect traffic.

Cuckoo spit on charlock or lodged in forks
of listing grass like frothy nebulae
we blow across softly to show the deity
within: little nymph; sheltered, sedulous
and still glassy as a grain of rice.
All day on a billion grains of quartz,

particles of shell, mica and glass,
or held in the surge of monadic glitter,
we find how our small bodies figure
rightly in the scale, and come back
up in sandals slapping melting tarmac
to a three-roomed house and four of us.

You stop and pluck your ballerinas,
twirl each in a pirouette and drop
them in your bucket, and trek back up
to set the dainty buds in sequences
around the stacks of fifty pences
on the sill there for the meter.

The sepals – the scarlet tutu of the dancer –
feel raw, like rubber, to the touch –
unlike the velvet of the amethyst
petals that petticoat the naked stems,
some several lengths of leggy stamens
tipped with black pumps, mid-entrechat ...

Limb by limb I amputate each flower
calmly, and gather up the stooks
in a Maguire & Paterson matchbox.
In time, this means you throw at me the vase
in which our father keeps his real matches
and I stay it there between us in mid-air.

Nick Laird

from THE CHORUS (ULSTER CYCLE)

Us left – the right, the wronged –
are told to hold our tongues
and pacts of silence rule
the graveyard, the packed bar,
the fields and cattle mart,
each segregated school

where given ink and time
history falls into line
and no-one mentions truth.
They insist that justice
can never rhyme with peace
so no, we can't have both.

We get the big-box store,
we get death's etcetera,
the physics of heartache
when she stops the engine
and stares out a slant rain
that falls with its own weight.

They say grief too passes,
collapses down in stages
much like the white marquee
we unstrung for folding
that fine day following
their anniversary.

Author's Note: These two poems were begun as responses to, respectively,
Seamus Heaney's 'The Haw Lantern' and his chorus from *The Cure at Troy*.

Annie Elizabeth Wiles

POST BREAK UP MORTEM

You stop hoovering,
but start wearing lipstick.

Saturdays suck.

Suddenly, Buffy the Vampire Slayer
is your best friend.

How long have you had this cereal?
It's hard to say.

Your apartment gets dirty
mysteriously.

You become a midnight philosopher.
What is life all about anyway?

You wonder if you should get a cat;
or maybe an iguana.

Am I a cliché? you wonder next,
then you wonder if this is why he's stopped calling.

You think about The Universe.
Upstairs, your neighbour begins to stalk you

with warm cans of European beer
at three in the morning.

Maybe you should move to Hawaii?
You buy a map.

Your tarot cards go in the bin.
You braid your hair

and look at yourself in the mirror.

Remember when you were a kid,

who made spaceships out of refrigerator boxes
and ate lucky pancakes,

and you just knew that anything,
anything at all could happen?

Annie Elizabeth Wiles

MODERN LOVE

He asks you out in bed.
You're strewn across it, woven
into the covers with a cigarette
and the book he's chosen.

It's midafternoon.
You're not wearing a bra –
you're a modern woman –
he's wearing his socks

but you like him anyway.
He puts down his phone
(he's serious today)
and asks you like: let's do this thing,

and you're like, yeah okay,
and then you're both like, cool.

Annie Elizabeth Wiles

IF ONLY

If only we could go back to college.
Hell, back then we could do anything, well,
you were failing math,
but anything other than that.

Just last year would be enough.
Back then we really achieved stuff;
we were really going places,
not just sitting around watching *The Office*.

Take me back to yesterday, even.
How easy things were back then!
Even about a minute ago, to be honest,
would be preferable to this.

A minute ago, we really had a chance,
if only you hadn't said, I fucked someone in France.

Annie Elizabeth Wiles

THINGS YOU SHOULD KNOW

The basics: I don't take milk in my coffee.
I hate walnuts, like really hate them,

and shouting,
and I hate being in love with you

and also, I don't like it
when you use my toothbrush.

Not caring how you cook my eggs this morning
does not mean I don't have opinions.

I care about a lot of things,
like the environment,

and like, the polar bears ...
But I care about you

more than anything else, somehow.
I care about your day

your childhood traumas
and what you had for lunch.

I care about your stupid car,
and when you don't come home.

You should have known I would care
about her, that I'd find out.

Belinda McKeon

THE BUSINESS OF LIVING

Conor O'Callaghan, *The Sun King* (The Gallery Press, 2013), €11.95.
Ciaran Berry, *The Dead Zoo* (The Gallery Press, 2013), €11.95.
Jen Hadfield, *Byssus* (Pan Macmillan, 2014), £9.99.

Faced with the subject of digital technology, most poetry squirms. Its
tropes are defiantly clunky, resistant to the muscle memory of a poem;
one part bizarre and two parts ridiculous, its verbs and its brand names
refuse to weave into a line to set it resonating in trusty, habitual ways.
They can transform what would otherwise have been perfectly passable
lyrics into Dad Rock. In other words, they raise the bar. The whole poem
has to be stronger in order to get away with them.

In his restless, interrogative fourth collection, Conor O'Callaghan
handles the question of twenty-first century communication as though it
were just one more folded MacBook, still quite warm. 'Lordship', his
opener, with its image of an 'antique Nokia' buzzing like tropical
wildlife, announces an intention to leapfrog familiar banks of imagery
and nostalgia in favour of less solid, dicier ground, and from this
confidence, these poems gain a brashness and a bruising energy which
propels them, and which – still more interestingly – occasionally trips
them up and tips them over into quieter, lonelier moments. In 'Required
Fields', a clever take on the online spaces we're forbidden to leave empty
if we want to proceed, 'these miscellaneous / undulating pewters we
keep returning to', the past is a thing closed into a storage space, and
unpacking it cannot be done without pain. In 'Three Six Five Zero', a
villanelle sprung from voicemail, old messages are 'blinking into a future
months complete'. 'Lordship' sets the collection's tone in more than one
sense, depicting as it does a character brooding and rattling his way
around a derelict house, his conscience bothered by slippages of commu-
nication both profound and mundane; he tries to catch 'scraps of signal
overspilling from the north', and ends up pleading forgiveness for an
inability to 'hack the secrecy', to 'go on outsourcing what history we
share', to 'breathe between it, / the "you" you truly were and spaced,
benighted me / already sentimental for the future's blown cover'.

A kind of stubborn inaccessibility is the prerogative these poems
frequently claim, their privacies coming across as coded and bruised; in
several poems, it's not clear whether the 'you' being addressed is the self
or another, but these explorations of identity, of alienation and of failure,
are all the more compelling for this. The collection, as the cover blurb

informs, is O'Callaghan's first in eight years, and the poems themselves seem conscious of the anxiety of a hiatus; not just in the sense of ferocious energy released (poems like 'The Server Room', 'Tiger Redux' and 'The Unfaithful Housewife' blister on the subjects of corporate jargon, the ruined Irish economy, and lust 'Filthy with soil and kisses'), but in the sense of recurring, knotty worry about poetry itself, about its ambitions and its shortcomings and indeed about the possibility that it can no longer be written. From a queasiness about metaphor in the short poem 'Wild Strawberries', to an imagining of poetry as gentrification in 'Translation' to the struggle with expression in 'Swell', in which a shower of blossoms on a windscreen demands to be written about, yet prompts doubt about both the impulse and the capacity to do so:

> All I mean to say is that it was lovely,
> that not every given is bleak or wrong
> and some even are as gorgeous as they are elementary.

The most beautiful poem in the collection is an elegy for things now rendered impossible, 'Kingdom Come', in the light of which all the swagger and jitter and insistence of almost every other poem in *The Sun King* are affectingly recast. The collection is named for an almost-stranger, a neighbourhood oddjob guy with 'transmission issues' – of the vehicular variety – whose self-possession inspires admiration but also a kind of longing: the longing to know, to be sure. 'Kingdom Come', with its air of too-late sadness, makes clear that this is a longing which can never be fulfilled, that it can never be 'evening over and over again'. And the business of living goes on.

Ciaran Berry's second collection, *The Dead Zoo*, is a display case of specimens studied and mulled over, several floors of such cases, in fact (the book runs to almost 90 pages). The epigraph from Diane Arbus ('I can hardly bear to leave any animal out') speaks to an apparently shared sense of completism on the part of the poet; these are poems often hectic with histories, exhibits and remembered moments caught in a queasy kind of aspic.

For Berry, who grew up in Ireland but has lived for several years in the USA, nostalgia seems an uneasy habit as much as it is a thematic inclination, and some of these poems wrestle with that habit, but some of them seem uncertain what best to do with its relics. For a poet only in his early forties, he deals, at times, in a backwards look reminiscent of a much older generation of emigrants; witness, for instance the 'broken rosary of tidy towns' that is Ireland in 'Reading the *Metamorphoses* on a Transatlantic Flight', but there is a more satisfying specificity to his glimpses of a 1980s childhood and adolescence; he imagines schoolchildren 'impatient for the home time bell, a car chase and cartoons' ('Schoolchildren, Cashelnagore'), and a DJ who speaks 'like he was raised in Malibu' ('Slow Set').

Berry has a sharp eye for the strange and the beautiful; in the title poem, a visit to Dublin's Natural History Museum reveals treasures caught in the 'swimming-pool blue of ... ethyl alcohol', a 'hamster reduced to just a house of bones', and 'whales suspended from the ceiling / like Calder mobiles in some art museum'.

History, myth, and biography, meanwhile, serve these poems also as an avenue of museums in which to wander and from which to pluck subjects to ponder more deeply. 'At Ballyconneely' evokes a 1908 mirage – a whole city – on the Connemara coast; 'All Things Bright and Beautiful' imagines the slow and careful writing of the famous hymn from the perspective of its creator; 'Slideshow' enacts a tender yet nervous sympathy with a parade of circus freaks. The poems are often marked by a patina of evident research: endnotes clarify the subject and references in several cases, weaving in moments from the work and lives of figures from Augustine to Einstein to Darwin. The studiousness lends them solidity, but perhaps ironically, it's when Berry allows his perspective to dart and hover over much more recent lived experience, as it does in the nervy 'Snipers, Anthrax, Dead Raccoons' – set during the days of the Beltway Sniper siege in 2002 – that his poems are at their most powerfully evocative.

The title of Jen Hadfield's third collection, *Byssus*, evokes a clinging – the word refers to the beard-like fibre by which a mussel attaches to the seabed – but also an anchoring, and many of Hadfield's striking, innovative poems explore the tension between these two modes of relation. Many of them take as their subject the poet's adopted place, Shetland, plunging often into the Shetland dialect (a brief glossary is provided), but they are poems as much about the look and the feel of language as they are about the look and feel of a place; 'aboutness', in the sense of finding and framing a poetic subject, is generally something with which, technically speaking, Hadfield's poems concern themselves in the most peripheral way. The opening poem, 'Lichen', for instance, is not 'about' the crusty fungus, vividly though it might describe its aspect ('The little ears prunk, scorch and blacken. / The little golden / mouths gape'); if it is about anything, it's about the mischief of describing lichen, about the things that lichen prompts a poet to do with words:

Who listens
like lichen listens
assiduous millions of black
and golden ears?

You hear
and remember
but I'm speaking
to the lichen.

Hadfield's stylistic inventiveness is rich, though it often seems more gleeful than formally purposeful; poems like 'the cockle's smile', 'The March Springs' and 'The Wedding Road, with Free Bar' cleave their cadences, and sometimes individual words, across the page so that any straightforward narrative delving is disrupted. A stronger disruptiveness lies in Hadfield's muscular resistance of the easily lyrical. She has a gift for brilliant images – in the prose poem 'Saturday Morning', she writes of 'milk from the freezer blown up into a yellow bagpipe', and of 'cockles in brine, mumbling sand and bubbling spires of mucus', while 'The Black Hole' describes the scattered feathers of a dead bird as being 'thickly leaved like pages / of a burnt book', 'a scuffed sequin of blood', a cat 'crunching into the ginger-nut' of the corpse. 'We climb the hill ... ', meanwhile, a poem about children on a nighttime hike, has a wonderful image of phones being cracked open 'like geodes', of attempts 'to take pics / of the stars, of dark country lanes, of the hot / perturbation of Sirius'. But it's when Hadfield pushes towards images less instantly vivid, less obviously *usable*, when her language achieves only a half-spokenness and a half-comprehensibility, when it becomes the eerie dialect not just of a place but of a mode of experience, that her poetry achieves the slow-burning dismantling of meaning that is its strength.

Matthew Campbell

THE ROAD LOOPS BACK

Peter McDonald, *Collected Poems* (Carcanet Press, 2012), £18.95.
Sam Burnside, *New and Selected Poems* (Ulster Historical Foundation,
2013), £9.99.

There is a moment in the poem 'Country', towards the end of this mid-
career *Collected Poems*, where Peter McDonald brings together his formal
attentiveness with a loose gracefulness. It's a simple effect, the poem
sounding the rhythm of the country waltz:

> The tight air overhead
>
> is jittery, alive,
> with music and pictures, voices
>
> all scrambled, but not dead,
> that pulse through years and places
>
> never remote again,
> and here I am *making believe*
>
> *I never lost you*, a one-two-
> one dance time, Patsy Cline
>
> steel-soft, not gone,
> the phrasing exact, heartbroken;
> my father and my mother
> still dancing to it, somewhere;
>
> all that, and the man
> on the road I left behind,
>
> bowed, put-upon,
> his head like mine

There is much skill in the workings of these lines: the delicate half-rhymes
across a three beat line that for all its looseness still retains the iambic as
its pulse; the wonderful counterpointed triple time of the country two-
step ('one-two- / one dance time'); the delicate musical connectedness of

assonance, 'voices' and 'places'; 'again' and 'one-two- / one' with 'Cline' and 'gone'; the musical resolution of these sounds in the dance of ghosts, 'my father and my mother / still dancing to it'; the stunning death-caesura before the gesture at the location of the dancing parents, 'somewhere'.

These tricks are of a higher mimesis, as might befit the classicism of a number of the poems which surrounded this poem in McDonald's 2011 *Torchlight* collection, and which have been a preoccupation of his poetry throughout his thirty-year publishing career. The presence of Patsy Cline; the racist, wife-strangling gospel singer Ira Louvin; and the little shafts of lyric from Roy Acuff or Hank Williams also suggest another aesthetic. This is a redneck culture, one part Appalachian and one part the great grim stretch driving through mid-Ulster. McDonald inevitably finds himself in a doubling relationship with place as one of a number of roads not taken, identities seemingly refused but still given a sort of haunting presence, like that 'man / on the road I left behind' (Robert Frost and Edward Thomas are never that far away from Elvis Presley and Willie Nelson in this autobiographical strain). If such identities are repudiated in McDonald's critical writing – to borrow the title of his collection of essays, they are *Mistaken Identities* – the poems play through the idea with a much more conflicted sense of where their writer has come from, what has been left behind, and a much more fragile sense of loss and disconnection.

The classical turn of his poems lends itself to satire and scorn, setting itself against contemporary poetry's perceived pieties with much of the rigour that has courted controversy in McDonald's criticism. His models are unerringly *elite*, for want of a better word: Homer and Virgil, Juvenal and Swift; in modern poetry not just MacNeice and Yeats, but also Eliot, Auden, Mahon, and Hill. In one way, this courting of classical and high-cultural models lends the poetry a clarity, a lexical and grammatical plainness which acts as a resistor to the difficulty which might ensue from such oppositions. In another, it lends a sense of self-questioning, a setting of the official statement against the actual experience of the poetry, which McDonald is a good enough reader of Yeats to know is the way to handle these things.

In 'The Road to Rome', for instance, McDonald gets as explicit as he ever does on a visit to the catacombs, inhabiting the sort of poised reflection of Mahon or late Eliot, a making it clear in patient syntax and thought:

> What meagre history I can bring
> down with me to these deathly streets
> restates, reiterates, repeats
> over and over the single rule
> taught in its hard and tedious school,

> how memory and firm belief,
> obliged at last to come to grief,
> perpetuate the old design,
> and always need to blur the line
> between hope and vanity.

So far, so thoughtful, with the satirist's slightly removed conception of religious convictions as both historical agency and distance. But the poet knows that he too shares the mystery, the sense of belief which can never be dismissed as mere 'hope and vanity'. A lengthy parenthetical digression can't hold itself back, cannot restrain, 'my bumptious Protestant / certainties and predispositions / – just call them foregone intuitions'. The speaker later calls himself 'an off-duty puritan' and 'colourblind'. The critic in McDonald would know that such a swerve back against a 'philosophical' understanding of the history of the place in front of him has long held a place both in the telling of histories of belief and its later incarnation as tourism.

In the dramatic or narrative poems in which he places his poet-speaker, McDonald shows the partiality of belief and the fracture in histories of place. The places in these poems extend from Belfast to Lisbon to Rome – and indeed a number are situated in Israel and Palestine, perhaps the most dangerous ground this poet of contested and broken places might tread. When he brings Israel back to the Braniel estate of his childhood, he knows the danger that is explicit in the scene-setting. The relation of these poems to the childhood place, the place of home, is one of perpetual revisiting and leaving again, a place never quite shucked off by versions of Homer or Virgil, even though that is another transplanting East from West. In 'Quis Separabit', seeing the Star of David flag flying in a sort of colonists' solidarity all over East Belfast (as it still does), McDonald phrases the flag as a question and not as a statement. From the Red Hand of Ulster to this:

> ... beside it – as clear as day – the Star
> of David, staunch beneath black skies,
> flown in defiance where it flies
> glaring into the backward mirror,
>
> surviving as one mote of white
> lodged like a flaw behind the eyes –
> white edged with blue. The message is
> a downright question: who will part
>
> blood from blood, and who desert us,
> daring to stand here, while we stand?

The road loops back, and has no end.
Here we remain and who shall part us?

This lyric is written in Tennyson's *In Memoriam* stanza, where the delayed echo of the outer rhymes stretches far enough apart to diminish accord, while the inner rhymes are held much faster together. In contrast, the content often presents difficult or complex material. The unionist planting of the Star of David flag, for example is an act of analogy; analogy, like rhyme, being the putting of two things together in difference. For all of their seeming parallels, these are irreconcilables, antinomial and at the limits of a rhetoric of similarity.

There are many other things to explore in this *Collected*: Peter McDonald also writes lyrics of nature and family, quite beautiful versions of classical eclogue and myth, and a number of travel pieces, friendship poems, elegies. He is also drawn to the parable and often, as in the lovely sequence 'The Pieces', the attractions of the modernist haiku-glimpse of the ephemeral. This material challenges in ways that do not shirk the difficulty of the task that the poet has set himself. The poems may displease a number of readers, since they do not offer easy understanding, and in their opening up of illiberal views, even court unpopularity. Frequently this doesn't read like poetry from Ireland, or even Northern Ireland; but for all its learning and historical grasp, and its cussed adherence to a difficult past and a present, it views as unreformable, the poetry is consistently drawn back to foregone intuitions forged in those places.

Derry poet Sam Burnside has collaborated with the Ulster Historical Foundation to produce a volume that is part *Selected Poems* and part a new sequence of animal poems, called 'Bestiary'. This latter is witty and light of touch, and in the tinier pieces it refreshes the allegorical bestiary of recent Northern poets like Muldoon. 'Wasps and Bees' is particularly pointed: 'Bees are more protestant than wasps.' Many of the poems in the earlier selection are occasional, offering brief moments of seeing, or fragments of autobiography and celebration of place.

The book's endpiece, 'From Grianaun of Aileach to Derry – December 21', is a poem about Christmas shopping, and also about the ancient monument on the road from Derry to Donegal. When he makes a poetic hit, as in this poem, Burnside matches the everyday with the historic, dodging the temptation to the specious sublime.

PETER SIRR INTERVIEWED BY AILBHE DARCY

Peter Sirr's collections with The Gallery Press are *Marginal Zones* (1984), *Talk, Talk* (1987), *Ways of Falling* (1991), *The Ledger of Fruitful Exchange* (1995), *Bring Everything* (2000), *Selected Poems* and *Nonetheless* (both 2004), *The Thing Is* (2009), and *The Rooms* (2014). A novel for children, *Black Wreath*, was published by O'Brien Press in 2014. His awards include the O'Shaughnessy Award for Poetry (1998) and the Michael Hartnett Award (2011). A member of Aosdána, he lives in Dublin where he works as a freelance writer and translator.

Ailbhe Darcy: For a little while recently you began to publish *Graph* again, the magazine you edited from 1986 to 1998 with Michael Cronin and Barra Ó Seaghda. It's a project that you've described as responding to a debilitating consensus in public debate and to the need for dissent. Is the same true of your poetry – do you feel that poetry has a role in dissent?

Peter Sirr: Well, you could argue that poetry is of its nature a form of dissent, an activity on the fringe of consensus. And of course we're all political beings, in lots of ways. But for me poetry doesn't necessarily come from a place of dissent as such; it may be there in some way, but it doesn't proceed from that, it doesn't start off as a political act in that direct or thought out or coherent kind of way. It's much more instinctive, emotional, imaginative. Often, the more ostensibly political a poem is, the less likely it is to succeed. If you start by saying, 'I want to write poems about ...', or 'I want to write an anti-war poem', the palpable design can destroy it. Yet, at the same time you are political, you feel of course that it's part of who you are as a person, so in some way that makes its way in. But it makes its way in a bit obliquely, I think.

AD: One way in which I would have thought of your poetry as political is in its interest in marginality: many of the characters in your first book are marginal, and of course the title of that first book is *Marginal Zones*.

PS: I was very interested then in lots of different kinds of marginality, whether it was specific marginal experience or the experience of language and marginality: the experience, for instance, in the Gaeltacht in the west. That sense of marginality. And also how, in a strange way, in Ireland, marginality is almost privileged; marginality is part of the Irish identity. So it was that, and also the feeling that poetry itself is a kind of marginal activity. And maybe it was a personal thing as well: maybe the sense that what is most interesting in life is often the thing that's most overlooked.

So the first book approaches marginality very rhetorically in some ways. There's the person who's left behind when the apostles out making their grand gestures, trying to lead an ordinary life after the event, that kind of aftermath. And there's the linguist in the Connemara Gaeltacht, studying the declining language, who's an interloper in this desolate, beautiful place that's too wind-blown to sustain even a tree. That first collection is very literary: it draws on a tradition of marginality. I started off with a sense of poetry as a slightly grand gesture, and I think that evolved over time into a preoccupation with margins in some way, but it's not exactly just that either – it gets complicated, because poetry is more to do with a quality of attention; you process your surroundings and realise what's important, what's interesting, or where you're going, in the course of the poem.

The essential question is always: what are you trying to do when you write a poem? You never set out to do something, you never sit down and say, *Right, I'm going to write about this or that.* You're trying to get beyond yourself, and beyond the immediately circumstantial, you're trying to realise something or to see into the heart of something. So whatever the ostensible subject of the poem is, *that* is what's going on, that attempt to get beyond it, to get to what is beyond.

AD: That takes me where I want to go, in a way, which is to religion. When we were talking earlier you said that you aren't religious, that your family isn't religious. Yet there is a sense of the immanent divine in your poetry, throughout your poetry. And while for the most part there aren't explicit references to religion in your poetry, there are moments where you explicitly turn to the culture, at least, of Christianity. In your first book, for example, there are those rewritings of Bible stories.

PS: Yes, I'm interested in the religious impulse. When I say I'm not religious, I suppose I dislike all organised religions, of every kind, and I wouldn't call myself a Christian. But I think anybody who's grown up in this country, in this culture, is saturated in years of aesthetic Christianity, and that interests me. And though I wouldn't want poetry to be a kind of ersatz religion, yet the impulse to create anything is religious in that it's an attempt to get beyond the self, it's an engagement with the cosmos in some way.

AD: In *Bring Everything*, 'Gospels' begins as a love poem to a woman, but moves into these various experiments in living, which seemed concerned with finding a way to live fully in the material world. I read it as a rethinking of the idea from Christianity that you have to divorce yourself from the world.

PS: Yes, that's what it is. I was interested in that kind of separation – partly, it's the Jesus story, and this idea that you must leave your life, that's how Christianity and other religions operate, you leave the world and go to this place that is somehow bigger than that. It's this question of leaving everything behind that I was interested in: the notion of rejecting a world in order to gain a world. I was playing with that idea and the forces resisting that. There's an imaginary male and an imaginary female figure, and a bit of a battle going on. On the one hand, ordinary reality and ordinary life, and on the other, this particular kind of spirituality that wants to leave everything, the unselfish impulse, I suppose. The poem asks, *Is it actually possible?* It's something that comes back in other poems; it comes back later on in 'Edge Songs'.

There are those lines, in 'Gospels', 'morning returns the world / we are gathered here / to refuse it' – you wake up and the world imposes all of its great reality on you, and you turn your back on it because you have a belief system. Most religions are built on denial, I suppose, or abnegation. This world is simply a trial that has to be undergone in order to get to the next one, whatever that is.

That's what the poem is resisting. And then it gets to the end, where it starts to play with that, with an alternative – instead of 'leave everything', this figure comes and says 'I want you to bring everything,' lovers, children, beasts, cheques, stubs, phone bills, and all the junk – that's the idea. That's really what's going on there. It's trying to find a way to live in the world with some kind of spiritual meaning but refusing to deny everything that makes life intense and rich and full.

AD: Eiléan Ní Chuilleanáin is another poet who's been very dedicated to the relationship between religious tradition and the material world; you've written about her and praised her.

PS: A great poet. Eiléan is a very pure poet in many respects. She creates these artefacts that are strange and surprising, and puzzling sometimes – each poem is some kind of enclosed system, a self-sustaining system. You're never quite sure: there are these voices coming and you're never quite sure where they're coming from, or quite what's being said.

AD: When you write about Ní Chuilleanáin, you praise her and Medbh McGuckian for their capacity to let the poem take them, to cede control to the poem. In your own process, is that how you work, or do you begin with a sense of the whole?

PS: When I'm reading a poem, that's the test that I would apply – that I expect a lot of people would apply. If you get to the end of a poem and you think that you could have predicted that from the beginning, then there's something not very interesting going on. It's better if you're forced to read something again much more slowly and think, how did that happen? How did I end up there? How did that journey work? The various trajectories of poems from a point to somewhere surprising and unpredictable – that's the job, in a way. That's what you hope would happen.

AD: Can you say a bit about 'China'? This poem is also in *Bring Everything*, and seems to contain an epiphany, a spiritual experience of some kind.

PS: It's partly a memory of childhood. I think one of the reasons I write a lot about the city is the sense of multiplicity. 'China' is about the sense of multiple lives taking place in the same space, and throughout time. There's that sense of thickly layered experience. History and archaeology are kind of an obsession for me, the sense that, if you lift up a paving, there are layers and layers of other experiences. The sense of routes, maps, cities, and all the journeys that have passed through them. And the sense that, you know, one individual life is never the full story, that it takes place in this kind of continuum of existence. And that walking in parallel with us through life are all the other people we've been in our own lives, all our other selves. The childhood self, which doesn't ever stop, which continues in parallel now with the older self.

The membrane between past and present is very thin and permeable. I suppose that's how memory works as well – memory is a constant admission of these other lives into the present. That's what I was on about, if you like, in the poem 'China', which doesn't really have much to do with China – the air seeming to thicken and another country pouring itself in, and suddenly you're transported somewhere else. Or it could be, as it was in this case, a simple memory of a childhood street in a different city, Waterford in fact, just a memory of walking down that street as a child. Again, a completely inconsequential thing that doesn't come announced. Or the sense that in any life there are moments when a door of perception, or whatever it is, opens and you can sort of see into things.

That's the way experience is, why should we think it's anything different? We see these portals into all kinds of other perceptions and experiences. That's what I meant by that sort of puzzling line at the end, the idea that we can't live singly any more than the 'light can fall on one place only'. We live multiply, inside of us.

AD: That idea of the city involving multiple worlds, multiple dimensions, and double lives, is found in a lot of postmodern novels – I'm thinking of Paul Auster's New York trilogy, for an example.

PS: I'm completely fascinated by cities and by fiction about cities. At the moment I'm writing a review of Italo Calvino's letters, so I've been reading *Invisible Cities* again, and I'm very taken by that book. It's one of my favourite books of his and in general.

I keep going back to the city as source of inspiration. Most recently in a poem like 'The Mapmaker's Song', which plays with notions of completeness and incompleteness, thinking of John Rocque's 1756 map of Dublin in which he claimed to have represented every single building in the city. And there are all kinds of great books about cities. B S Johnson's first novel, *Albert Angelo*, about a supply teacher in London, is a fascinating look at that city. There's a whole radical English poetic tradition as well, people I really like, such as Roy Fisher – the Birmingham he doesn't write *about* but tries to write *with*. I love that idea, of writing *with* the city.

There are all sorts of Irish people, too – everything from *Ulysses* onwards, there's a great radical Irish tradition of writing about and with cities: Joyce, Kavanagh, McGahern, Kinsella of course, Trevor Joyce, MacNeice, Clarke ...

AD: Your interest in the city often centres around completeness and incompleteness: plans for the city that never come to fruition, architects' designs that never get built, or plans that don't work out as they should, such as the spire that has to be lopped off the church because it's too tall and makes the city authorities uncomfortable.

PS: There was a website called Dublin Unbuilt, it was created by architects and it showed plans for all these great buildings that were going to be built, a new cathedral that was going to be at the end of Capel Street, or whatever. They were drawn and planned for but just never made it, and I became really interested in these – it's a kind of alternative world scenario. There's something magical about cities because you can never define what is a city, the built environment and the human one. It is impossible. I used to live in different cities, in Milan and so on, and I used to constantly patrol them and try to get at them and understand them in some way. And I'd realise that each city is a deeply personal experience: everybody's city is a different city.

People forget that in Ireland sometimes, because our notion of *dinnseanchas* tends to be wrapped up in the experience of the home place, and we're very good at that, but it's a specific kind of geographically defined space, whereas a city is a dynamic, shifting series of spaces that you don't necessarily possess. I set out most mornings and I walk the length of the Grand Canal, and I think: this is my neighbourhood because I've made it my neighbourhood with my feet. It might not necessarily be my neighbours' neighbourhood, because they might not go there, they might go off in the other direction, or their neighbourhood might be the few streets where they live. So everyone has a different city. I'm fascinated by that.

AD: Earlier you were resisting the idea that you're a political poet, and yet this seems to me like a fundamentally political idea – the idea that an individual can rewrite the city, can create within a system.

PS: I don't know why, but I've spent a lot of time in the last few years thinking about that while I've been trying to write prose. I've been writing prose essays about the city and about trying to understand what the city means, and about what my experience of it means. And also looking at the history of the past of the city, looking at specific city streets and their past. Just trying to arrive at some kind of understanding of the individual's relationship to a city.

I suppose I have a lot of views and, I suppose, angers as well about what has happened to, or what happens to, cities in Ireland – our distrust of them. Which is all changing, because I think young people have a very different attitude to cities now, but when I grew up there was an utter distrust of the urban, the urban was dangerous. The city centre was where districts were poor, or where people were just provisionally passing through. The ideal was suburban or rural, and that's what the establishment prized. So the inner core was left to rot for so long. And very gradually we moved away from that and started to prize it again. But we still don't prize it enough, I think. So I do, on that level, have lots of feelings about that, comparing cities in Ireland with other cities and getting a sense of what it could be like, you know when you go to Berlin or Amsterdam or Copenhagen or elsewhere ... And yet there's this huge energy that Dublin has, that isn't like other places.

AD: Compared with *Bring Everything*, the next book, *Nonetheless*, is a relatively celebratory collection, there's a sense of settling down in it. I wonder if you're tracing in some way the boom and then the bust.

PS: Well, the personal takes place in the context of the social, and I went to live in the centre of the city when there was this huge explosion of building developments and so on in the mid-nineties, and you couldn't but be aware of that. On the one hand you were hit by the past, and on the other hand this contemporary grasping. I was very much aware of that, and it leaked into the writing. I'm not sure about 'celebratory' though; I always think that in some ways I'm far too restless to be blindly celebratory, so I'm not sure if *Nonetheless* is different in that sense to *Bring Everything*. I think there are moments in both collections that would resist a crude greed.

AD: 'The Overgrown Path' in *The Thing Is* has joy in it – it's about the birth of your daughter – but there are also poems like 'PPS', which are more sinister, where you're giving her up to the state.

PS: These are things that everybody feels, I'm sure. 'PPS' is about that moment when the postman drops in a letter, and it's the assignment of the PPS number, the state's first intervention in her life. It's the intersection of the social with the personal. You're going kind of googly-eyed with love for this little creature, and you realise she's the state's creature as well. Again it's that thing of all these complex systems that are working away behind us. 'The Overgrown Path' – the title came from Janáček – was about a series of moments of power in a way, although really it's a series of instinctive responses. Because a child is such a big experience in your life, your own life is so changed by it, and the consciousness out of which you're writing changes. Everything is different. You've got a new perspective, and a new set of fears. There are all sorts of paradoxical impulses about that. There's an intensity to it all; the child's own first experiences, her first encounter with everything. You realise how a child sees everything differently, you envy that, want to be like that.

AD: The form that 'The Overgrown Path' takes, the sequence of short poems, is one that you return to again and again in your collections. Is it the openness of this form that you're interested in? That it resists closure somehow?

PS: It's a strange thing because I know I do that a lot; it's not even a designed thing, necessarily. And 'sequences' is probably the wrong word for me, in the sense that a lot of them aren't particularly sequential. I think of them more as gatherings of related impulses – that they talk to each other, the different parts often talk to each other. In the new book, *The Rooms*, there's a long sequence again, or a gathering of sonnets which all talk to each other. It's that Rimbaud sense of a poem never being finished but abandoned. It's that sense of trying something, of coming at it from another angle. Maybe it's a kind of indecisiveness – I know there's something there, but I haven't got at it yet. It's a dangerous kind of thing, I've done this in lots of books – 'A Journal' in *The Ledger*,

Saoirse Wall, living and working between Dublin and Mayo

Still from *Gesture 2*, 2014
HD video

Shortlisted, Hennessy Portrait Prize 2014

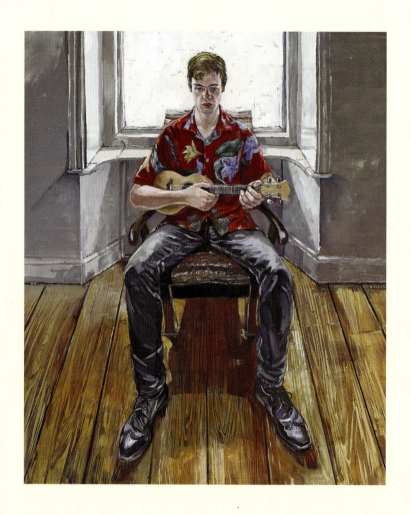

Una Sealy, from Dublin

Hibiscus Blues (Portrait of Douglas), 2014
Oil on canvas, 120 x 100 cm

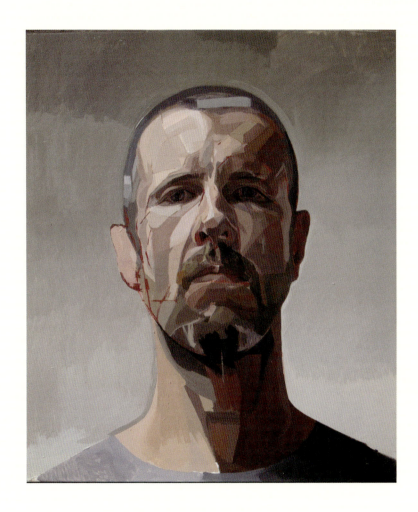

Gavan McCullough, from Co Meath

This, 2014
Oil on canvas, 70 x 60 cm

Shortlisted, Hennessy Portrait Prize 2014

Nick Miller, from London, resident in Ireland for many years, now based in Sligo

Last Sitting: Portrait of Barrie Cooke, 2013
Oil on linen, 61 x 56 cm

Winner, Hennessy Portrait Prize 2014

Thanks to The National Gallery of Ireland for permission to use these images.
All portraits are on show in The National Gallery until 8 February 2015.

there's the 'Edge Songs', 'Death of a Travel Writer' in *Ways of Falling*, there's also the Catullus in *The Thing Is*.

So, yes, it's the openness. The closed, conventional lyric poem isn't necessarily always the right form or hugely interesting, and though I do write short self-contained poems as well, there is something about open forms or undecided forms that attracts me. It's about excitement and the sense that it's a journey: there are points along the journey that you want to visit, but you don't know how it's going to end. That's how it happens, but sometimes I resist it and I resent it and I go back and try to write a short little poem. So again the new book is a combination of all these kind of contradictory impulses.

AD: Are the sonnets rhymed?

PS: They're not really, no. They're not proper sonnets. There's lots of internal rhyme going on, but they're not really conventional sonnets, they're fourteen-line poems pretending to be sonnets. I'm actually very interested in the craft, the making of a poem. I'm very interested in the possibilities of form, in shape and sound and measure, and I'm very conscious of the poem as a sound event and a visual event, an artefact built out of language. I have no interest in fetishising particular approaches or privileging one set of formal gestures over another. I like different kinds of poetry – I like formal poetry, I love Robert Graves, Thomas Hardy, Yeats, but I'm also deeply interested in the traditions that disrupt conventional form. I love Oppen and the Objectivists, stretches of Pound, Olson's Maximus poems, Ed Dorn, or the questing kind of reinvention of people like Andrea Zanzotto or Anne Carson or Michael Haslam. I love what Jean Follain does, or Jacques Réda or Francis Ponge, and Roy Fisher, John Riley, Denise Riley, Brecht, Bishop – a pretty eclectic mix. I want everything in a way. I want to be able to use it all.

AD: Your poetry refuses to reconcile itself to either of the two 'camps' in Irish poetry, if you like. On one level your work is very much in the experimental, modernist tradition – but then it disqualifies itself completely by insisting on a coherent subject position, a lyric 'I'.

PS: Yes, I'd be thrown out of most postmodernist poetry conferences for that! And I'd be thrown out of the other camp for being too messy. But again, your context – I've always resisted that notion of 'Irish poetry' because I find it boring and limiting. I hate the way in which things get viewed within a particular sort of national framework, which is often an identitarian kind of framework. For instance, you're setting yourself up to have less attention paid to you if you don't write about ostensibly Irish subject matter. You don't write about the famine or you don't write about the North, or whatever it's going to be. There are all these expectations around what makes an Irish poet, and I don't think of myself even as an Irish poet, if you take that as a phrase, because an awful lot of the people I'm interested in aren't even Irish. We all construct our own traditions, and the tradition I've constructed for myself is what I identify with more than an Irish tradition. Equally, I'm not very interested in the mutual exclusivity and boring self-righteousness of 'camps'. These divisions are about power rather than poetry, about dividing up the meagre spoils and trying to create little bastions of privilege.

AD: And yet in 'Edge Songs' you do court thinking about this divided or lost or fragmented Irish literary tradition.

PS: Yes: I have been interested in that from the beginning. One of the poems in that first book is 'The Collector's Marginalia', about a linguist going to somewhere like Connemara and collecting the language. Which is why, years later, when I came across Mark Abley's book *Spoken Here*, which is a kind of travel book where he visits endangered languages, I was very interested in that.

I went to a school where Irish was despised, where four people in the class were doing honours Irish or were interested in it. The discovery of Irish, if you like, was very important to me at the time, and I decided to go to university and study it, and immerse myself in Irish literature. 'Edge Songs' is a kind of a recovery of my own tradition; it came out of going back and re-reading that early Irish poetry and poetry in Latin, there's a great tradition of Irish poetry written in other languages and Irish poetry that is about wandering abroad but also writing – I was playing with that idea as well. And I translate a good bit of poetry from Irish, so I have an engagement with that.

All poetry, all writing, comes out of a sensibility, in that you can only write the poems that you can write. And whatever tradition you come out of, it's in some sense predetermined. You don't consciously hunt out things because they'll be exciting to you. They're exciting to you because you have a particular sensibility. Your tradition is in part conscious, in part instinctive, in part using the things around you that you're excited about or interested in.

That's what happens. No one operates within a single framework, or if you do it's boring. And I suppose I've seen a bit of that as an editor, where people will only write a single kind of poem and think that's what being an Irish poet is.

AD: Do you think of yourself as writing to an Irish audience?

PS: I don't really have a developed sense of an audience at all. Prose has an audience, but as a poet you have a couple of fanatical followers maybe, if you're lucky. Your audience is first of all yourself. You may have experienced this yourself Ailbhe, with your own first book – there may be a small number of people who buy the book and an even smaller number who actually read it. But poetry's a long game – I do believe that. Most things will disappear, it's true; but in the same way that you have a conversation with a tradition, because you're reading poems that are thousands of years old, maybe one poem of yours will survive.

Ailbhe Darcy's travel costs from South Bend, Indiana to Dublin to interview Peter Sirr were partly funded by a Krause fellowship from the American Conference for Irish Studies (ACIS).

Peter Sirr

RIFF FOR BEATRIZ
  – for and after Beatriz de Dia, *trobairitz*, 12th century

Ab joi et ab joven m'apais

I feed on joy and youth   the rest
forget   all texts
abandoned   I feed
with joy   I feed on you or would
were you here   were I there
by the lake   in the wood   where the
nightingales are   I hear them
the buds along the branches roar
the frost withdraw   I feast on the season
that you may come to me
like light to the trees   I set
my pilgrim heart to roam
I am here   your loosened armour your
Saracen hands   I feed
on spices and desert air
the rest is argument   discourse
the lines unwinding
the lines bound like the twigs of a broom
to sweep you away and pull you back
my dust is yours together we blow through the meadows
I was here but now
a stir of language in the trees   birdsong
in the composed season   a voice
before the frost comes   before the wind and the rains
bear me off   come to me please

Peter Sirr

WHEN THE SWEET AIR TURNS BITTER

Quant l'aura doussa s'amarzis

When the sweet air turns bitter
and the leaves fall from the branches
when the birds shift languages
I shift with them, singing hard
love which hounds me, holds me close
who never had the least power over it.

What could I have had from it
or ever expected but
the prescribed torment
since what I want is the one thing
I can never possess.
Longing's where I live, what I touch:

there's a strange joy in it
the hard jewel, incorruptible
desire. It cannot say its name
I can't speak a word when I see her.
In my mind I speak. When
she's gone I speak: no-one should listen then.

No-one compares. The paragons
the most beautiful ever   take them
they are not worth a glove.
When the world darkens she
still shines, breath in my body to see it
Christ, to see her body shine.

So I burn I tremble so I am
startled whether sleeping or waking
for love of her I am afraid
I might die yet can say nothing
but I will serve her two years or three
and then she'll know the truth.

Not dead, nor alive, nor do I
recover or feel what I suffer.
I can't tell love's future
if she'll love me or when
only she has the pity   no-one else
can raise me up or let me fall.

When she maddens me I dance
or stand openmouthed like a fool
it is my pleasure to be laughed at
mocked to my face or whispered about
because after the bad will follow the good
and quickly follow if it pleases her.

If she won't have me, then I should have died
on the first day of my servitude.
God, how sweetly she struck me down
when I saw love's semblance
so locked in the prison of her eyes
I can never look elsewhere.

Miserable, still I rejoice
for if I shrink from her or court her
then I'll be true or I'll be false
as she likes it   faithful or tricksy
rough and ready or all courtly
trembling or cool and easeful.

She can do with me what she wants

and so I say, I, no-one, Cercamon
he is no courtly man, or ever can be
who despairs of love.

Author's Note: Cercamon, twelfth century, was one of the earliest
troubadours. Cercamon means 'world searcher' in medieval Occitan.

Peter Sirr

AFTER BORGES

1. *To a minor poet*

Where are the days you spent on earth,
all the joy and anguish
that were your universe?

The river of years has washed them away;
now you survive
as an entry in the index.

Proudly they gather, the gods' gifts, immortal.
Of you, dark friend, all we know
is that one evening you heard the nightingale.

Walking fields of asphodels, your slighted shade
must think the gods harsh
but the days are a tangle of paltry needs

and is there really a blessing richer
than the ash of which oblivion's made?
For others the gods kindled

a persistent light: see
how it shines in every crevice, finds every flaw
and in the end shrivels the rose it treasures.

They were kinder to you, brother, passing you by,
leaving you to the nightingale in the garden
in the thrill of a dusk which will never darken.

2. *To the son*

It wasn't me who fathered you, it was the dead:
my father, his father, their fathers before them
tracing their way through a maze of loves
all the way from Adam, from the deserts
of Cain and Abel, a dawn so distant
mythology blocks the view. And here
they are now: flesh and bone, their feet
in the future, their breath on your shoulder.
They crowd around, I can feel them press,
we, you, those yet to come, the sons
you'll conceive, the latest of the line,
the red line of Adam, and I am
all the others too, eternity hurrying
in the bones of time ...

3. *To a Saxon poet*

The snows of Northumbria have felt
and forgotten the print of your feet
and the nights are uncountable that lie
between us, my ghostly brother.
Slow in the slow dark you'd work
your metaphors of swords on the seas,
the horror in the pine woods
and the loneliness the days brought.
Where should we look for your face
and your name? In the halls of oblivion.
I'll never know how life was for you
when you were a man on the earth,
you who followed the hard paths of exile
and now live only in iron verses.

4. *A compass*

Everything comes down to a word in a language
someone or something, night and day,
is writing in an infinite confusion.
This is the history of the world, Carthage

and Rome, you, me, everyone, my life
which is beyond me, its torment
of chance, mystery and secret codes
and all of Babel's discords.

Behind the name the nameless lies,
today I felt its shadow settle
in the clear blue compass needle

stretching to the limit of the seas,
like a clock seen in a dream
or a bird suddenly moving in its sleep.

Belinda Cooke

CLOSE READINGS

Edited by Richard Rankin Russell, *Peter Fallon: Poet, Publisher, Editor and Translator* (Irish Academic Press, 2014), €20 hb.
Leontia Flynn, *Reading Medbh McGuckian* (Irish Academic Press, 2014), €20 hb.

Richard Rankin Russell's *Peter Fallon: Poet, Publisher, Editor and Translator* will be a revelation for aspiring writers who see established poetry presses as impregnable citadels rather than the small dedicated outposts that they very often are. This book of tributes celebrates Peter Fallon's major contribution to Irish poetry as founding editor of Ireland's foremost poetry publisher, The Gallery Press, while showing him also to be an inspiring role model who, though a poet of the first order himself, is happy to leave his poetry light under a bushel while he acts as a catalyst for numerous successful careers. Unlike George Bailey in Frank Capra's 1946 Christmas classic, Fallon, it seems, didn't need an angel to convince him that 'It's a wonderful life': as Shaun O'Connell notes: '[H]e has shaped an exemplary and coherent life combining poetry with his living cares'. There is something strangely comforting in reading about this life, which, even in the face of personal loss, continues to do what it set out to do.

Seamus Heaney – while noting Peter's partner Jean Fallon's shared running of the press – cites Fallon's own words in the introduction to a souvenir booklet celebrating Gallery's fortieth anniversary:

> We uphold twin imperatives – to keep the art of poetry (and its
> relationships with its audience) alive and in good health, and to celebrate
> it because its tradition is essential to our culture, and because, by
> participating in it, we may refine our capacities to think and feel. We
> may, in short, learn to think and feel better.

Rankin Russell tracks Gallery back to the watershed year of 1972, when a number of established writers moved to the press, a development Fallon described as an 'act of "retrieval" of Irish works', an act he now sees 'as one of the subtle revolutions in Gallery's existence'. The editor concludes his Introduction with an outline of the book's contents (which include a history of the press, articles on Fallon's poetic development, his nature poetry, his American connections, and poems in his honour), as evidence of Peter Fallon's fostering of 'a living literary community in Ireland that has over-spilled the boundaries of gender and generation, province and nation, and reached the shores of Britain and America'.

The history of the press is a great way to begin Fallon's own story – a nostalgic, heady, reliving of fledgling years in Dublin as a 'mover and shaker', painted vividly by Dennis O'Driscoll: 'His dashing dress code and exuberant spillage of ink-black hair lent him an aura that was as dandyish as it was hippyish, as mystical as it was modish' ('Peter Fallon Revisited'). Thomas Dillon Redshaw gives us a whirlwind social history from the Beatles' Dublin concert (1963) through to the 'bomb culture' of the Troubles, amidst the Dublin Arts Festivals (1970/71), tracking Fallon and Eamon Carr's eight Tara Telephone (originally their band name) chapbooks up to the first Gallery text – Pearse Hutchinson's *Watching the Morning* (1972). He even covers Fallon's apprenticeship in print craft: 'an introduction to a craft-conscious readership both aware of "the book beautiful" and mindful of a national tradition'.

Fallon's relocation of the press from Dublin to Loughcrew, Co Meath is fundamental to his poetic development. Here, until very recently, he combined publishing with running a sheep farm. Maurice Harmon overviews Fallon's writing, emphasising his insider/outsider experience as both farmer and poet. In *The Speaking Stones* (1974) he shifts from his early love themes to Loughcrew itself, where 'Farm work became a metaphor for the work of poetry' ('Peter Fallon's Profane Rituals'), celebrating both farming and small-community life, whilst not denying the downside and social penalties of rural living.

> ... I think it exquisite
> to stand on the yard, my feet on the ground,
> in cowshit and horseshit and sheepshit.
>   – 'WINTER WORK'

John McAuliffe stresses Fallon's nuanced interweaving of nation and place in contrast to Paul Muldoon's 'hallucinatory narratives', citing Martin Gale's paintings as similarly oblique, where 'human figures rarely face the viewers, turning away and looking at something out of shot'. Thomas O'Grady's discussion of Fallon's 2004 adaptation of Patrick Kavanagh's novel *Tarry Flynn* introduces us both to Kavanagh's wonderful, conflicted Tarry, for whom place, 'even while capturing the heart also has the potential to imprison the soul', along with Kavanagh's own modest self-assessment: 'not only the best but the only *authentic* account of life as it was lived in Ireland this century ... I have closed the door on that class of a novel – no one for a generation will attempt to write about the Irish countryside.'

Ed Madden's in-depth research focuses on Fallon's powerful lyric poetry about the death of his baby son John shortly after birth, on 8 December 1990, poems referenced by many of the contributors:

Some take life hard,

    some take the same life
    easy. I'd sooner sing
    heartbreak nor cry it.
    But a baby's born, the baby
    dies. Who knows anything.
        – 'A WAY OF THE WORLD'

Madden's essay analyses the sequence within a structuralist framework, as well as examining Irish gender differences on grief, and the particular problem of young male suicides, possibly exacerbated by male suppression of emotion.

Shaun O'Connell takes us on a walking tour of Loughcrew as, gifted with wellies, he accompanies Fallon on his rounds – 'a man who knew who he was and where he was'. Rankin Russell then frames Fallon's work within environmental literacy criticism, while noting the key influence of Wendell Berry whom Fallon describes as 'the most wise and thoughtful man I know'. Justin Quinn examines Fallon's shifting narrative voices as central to his own voice within the community, using the poem 'If Luck Were Corn' as an example of 'the process of moral adjustment that takes place in personal interactions in the community'. Joseph Heininger show-cases extracts from Fallon's translation of Virgil's *Georgics*, along with close textual analysis to evidence Fallon's skill as translator.

The final two essays take us to America where Joyce Peseroff examines Fallon's commissioned poem on Deerfield Academy, where he has taught, followed by Bryan Giemza's piece on Fallon's lifelong friendship with Wendell Berry, described here as a sensitive and religious man. The section concludes with Berry's preface to Fallon's *Airs and Angels,* which nicely pins down an objective quality noted by many of the contributors, involving 'a kind of propriety, a kind of modesty, by which the subject is granted a precedence over the poet'.

Once we work through the little 'gallery' of dedicatory poems Rankin Russell has included, one is left with the sense of a delightful 'This Is Your Life' anthology, which acts both as a tribute to Fallon as poet and also as a validation of the editing and publishing life, inspiring readers to, in Fallon's words: 'improve our chances of fulfilling ourselves individually and collectively as a human, decent, kind society'.

Also testifying to the Irish Academic Press's aim to bring quality texts before a wider audience is Leontia Flynn's *Reading Medbh McGuckian,* offering further insights for admirers of McGuckian's poetry and affording a means to reconnect for those put off by the opacity of her later work. Flynn gives an endearing (occasionally funny) 'heart on her sleeve' account of how an initial passion for 'what is witty, challenging and genuinely radical about McGuckian's work', changed to frustration mid-Ph.D., after Shane Alcobia-Murphy's research into McGuckian's substantial subtextual referencing. As McGuckian herself relates: '[L]ike a bird building a nest ... I gather materials over the two weeks, or whatever'. Flynn is more than a match for McGuckian's wizardly postmodernist machinations in the context of *l'écriture feminine*, but less engaged when working with labyrinthine references to Russian writers such as Osip Mandelstam, Boris Pasternak, and Marina Tsvetaeva, along with nineteenth-century women's biographies and Irish political histories.

Flynn's introduction explains her continued love of McGuckian's early 'rich, strange, luminous, poetry ... filled with resonances of a vital, lived life', set against her disillusionment with the 'diminishing returns' of the later, prolific, cut-and-paste outpourings. She notes McGuckian's gifted arrival onto the poetic stage with her National Poetry Competition winner of 1979, 'The Flitting', where 'image proliferates on image, finally telescoping beyond the "well-earthed" speaker as well as beyond the reader's understanding', an approach that gradually triggered mystified, dismissive responses from the (often male) establishment. Typical of these were James Simmons who declared her a 'hoax', and Patrick Williams, who thought it 'pseudo poetry', with the poet possessed of 'counterfeit authority'. Flynn responds: 'Some reviewers even suggested that since poems like 'The Flitting' channelled deep reserves of mysterious femininity, they, as men, were unequipped to respond to them – and so off they went, presumably to read something else instead.' Examples of McGuckian's amusingly contradictory elucidations of her own work only added fuel to the fire. Above all, here, Flynn perceptively makes plain McGuckian's postmodernist intent, along with ample evidence of how many critics failed to grasp that McGuckian's 'irony and a fondness for postmodern trouble-making' were all part of a feminism which included the juxtaposition of stereotyped feminist personas.

Flynn's early chapters offer astute analysis of selected poems. Chapter One looks in detail at common misinterpretations of McGuckian's various female selves as versions of her own subjectivity. She argues convincingly for the radical nature of McGuckian's feminism, showing how she moved on from Adrienne Rich and Eavan Boland's earlier innovations of placing women at the centre of their poetry. In her collection *The Flower Master* (1982) and the pamphlet, *Single Ladies* (1980), she takes women's poetry a step further: creating 'ironic deployments of the caricatures into which women writers have too easily been allowed to fall: sullen spinsters, writers of railway novels, super-feminine purveyors of unprivileged genres like Romance, gothic tulip-governesses.'

Chapter Two looks at how French feminist theory has informed *Venus and the Rain* (1984), discussing Hélène Cixous's focus on female language,

Lucy Irigaray's consideration of the body, and Julie Kristeva on semiotics. In a useful application of literary theory to contemporary poetic output, Chapter Three looks at how Alcobia-Murphy's subtextual revelations of the nineties inform *On Ballycastle Beach* (1988), while Chapter Four is a substantial approach to *Marconi's Cottage* (1991), McGuckian's house, where in 1898 Guglielmo Marconi experimented with radio waves. These radio waves offer a particularly pertinent metaphor for the proliferation of sub-texts that McGuckian draws on from this point in her work. Flynn seeks out lines (or waves) of connection between biographies (of Gwen John, Emily Brontë, and Tatyana Tolstoy's biography of her father), and a wide range of memoirs, letters and critical texts on Russian writers, to the extent that the list of cited and applied wave-texts may well be in danger of drowning the unguarded reader (and the by now guarded author). By the end of this discussion, Flynn comes close to losing all patience with (and certainly all pleasure from) McGuckian's work.

> Such connections could expand beneath or around the poems as they did in *Marconi's Cottage*, to the point where the poem is more or less forgotten, if it is still relevant at all. These meanings then can now surely only fully be understood or *remembered* by the author herself. Moreover, none of this has anything to do with poetry ...

Flynn has provided a highly intelligent study of a complex poet which includes a comprehensive survey of McGuckian's intertextuality, of benefit to a general reader less familiar with academic readings of McGuckian's work. Somewhat ironically, given Flynn's ultimate impatience with McGuckian's later (and, we assume, future poetry), this book may well encourage lapsed McGuckian readers to brave once more some of her more mystifying lines, with the benefit of Flynn's insights and subtextual discoveries.

Liam Carson

A BIRD IN AIR

Colette Ní Ghallchóir, *An tAmharc Deireannach / The Last Look* (Arlen House, 2014), €15.
Francis Harvey, *Donegal Haiku* (Dedalus Press, 2013), €11.50.
Mark Roper, *A Gather of Shadow* (Dedalus Press, 2012), €10.50.

People and place, poverty and power – these are just some of the themes in Colette Ní Ghallchóir's poetry. She explores how landscape and community shape the individual, and her work is replete with images from her native area, the Bluestack Mountains in Donegal, noted for its storytellers and fiddlers. Her poems are sparse, taut, marked by a startling and often disarming directness. As Cathal Ó Searcaigh points out in his introduction to *An tAmharc Deireannach / The Last Look*, a bilingual selection of work from her collections *Na Síoga i Lag na hAltóra* and *Idir Dhá Ghleann*, they are 'plain without being prosaic'.

Ní Ghallchóir's landscapes are infused with family memory and folklore. In the poem 'Spiorad mo Chine' (translated by Denise Blake as 'Spirit of My Clan'), she seeks 'coiscéimeanna mo mhuintire' ('traces of my forebears'). She finds her ancestors 'blow through the rowan trees / abundant with fruit' ('ag seideadh tríd chrann caorthann / trom le torthaí'). In 'Fios', a woman dies, and her stories vanish into the grave – 'anois tá gach dáimh / gach scéal / sa chill'.

There is, however, nothing sentimental about Ní Ghallchóir's work. Many of her poems feature marginalised or rejected men and women. Her community can be harsh and judgmental. In 'Clog an Phobail', a woman is read out from the altar, and driven 'ó phobal go pobal'. 'Ar an Imeall' (translated by Gabriel Rosenstock as 'On the Edge'), finds the poet in the guise of a 'mountainy goat' ('gabhar an tsléibhe'), 'that dwells on the edge of the peak':

> scartha amach
> ó mo chairde a d'fhág mé
> in uair na cinniúna.

> cut off / from the companions that deserted me / in my hour of need.

In 'An Bhallóg', a woman describes herself as a ruined house, and the poem is charged with images of desolation and emptiness:

mo shúile a bhí lonrach
dorcha,
mo dhíon titithe isteach

In 'Éalú' ('Escape'), the individual seeks release from the constrictions of a community defined by 'lucht na cúlchainte' ('the backstabbing gossips'). In a poem dedicated to neglected Donegal poet Madge Herron, she again evokes 'cúlchaint', variously translated by Gabriel Rosenstock in his elegant English version as 'prattle' and 'malicious talk'. She speaks of Herron's 'broken body' ('do chorp briste'). The very landscape is charged with darkness and death, as in 'An tUbh Briste' (rendered by Rody Gorman as 'The Lossbroken Egg', where she sees 'the skullshell lossbroken in smithereens' ("feicim an bhlaosc, briste 'na smionagar").

Ní Ghallchóir also probes power relationships and the betrayals within personal relationships. There is the child abused by a priest in 'Roghnaithe' (translated by Joan Newmann as 'Chosen'); the servant girl of 'Buíochas' (rendered by Frank Sewell as 'Thanks a Lot'), who eats 'the crumbs that fall from the master's table' ('na grabhrógaí / a thiteann ó thábla an mháistir'; and the heartless husband of 'An Fear Uasal' ('The Gentleman'), 'lán den fhuacht folaithe / a bhí i ndán dom' ('full of the concealed cold / that was to be my fate').

The English translations – or versions, it would be more correct to say in some instances – take varying approaches. Gabriel Rosenstock, Celia de Fréine and Nuala Ní Dhomhnaill adhere closely to the forms and structures of the original Irish texts, avoiding any gimmickry that might blur the clear tone of Ní Ghallchóir's voice. Rody Gorman adopts the tactic of creating compound words that attempt to capture the complex shades of meaning in seemingly simple Irish words and phrases. Hence 'an saol mór' becomes 'the greatbig secularlifeworld'; 'droim' becomes 'ridgeback'; and 'ar an bhealach' becomes 'on the soundroadway'. Joan Newmann's versions take the greatest liberties, often creating what are effectively new poems that riff off the original poems, with mixed results. Her version of 'Roghnaithe' adds a haunting tone to the original, but her version of 'An Bhallóg' bears little relation to Ní Ghallchóir's poem, losing much of its power, not least in the title itself, where 'Homeplace' has a meaning very much at odds with 'An Bhallóg'.

Ní Ghallchóir's gorgeous little poem 'Mo Chóta' tells of 'an outworn cloakrag' of a coat, but could very easily be about the Irish language that she has chosen as her mode of expression. It carries echoes of Nuala Ní Dhomhnaill's 'Ceist na Teangan' :

ach tá línín ann
den tsíoda is fearr
a chlúdaigh droim prionsa ariamh.

But it's lined / with the finest silk / that ever covered the ridgeback of a prince.

'In poetry it's the concrete image that appeals to me most of all. I try to avoid abstraction. It's entirely possible to achieve that effect. I try for clarity with mystery. Clarity on its own is not enough, you also need mystery; the reader must work a little as well.' So declared the recently deceased Francis Harvey. Like Colette Ní Ghallchóir, his poetry is inextricable from the Donegal landscapes in which he made his home. And, indeed, there are striking echoes to be found in the work of these two poets. Take these lines from Harvey's 'The New Scholars':

> They had no eye for the light on high ground
> could see enough with the light in the glen.

And compare with these lines from Ní Ghallchóir's 'Na Cnoic':

> Fanóidh mé sna hísleáin
> i bhfad ó pharrthas bhur screigeanna.

> I'll stay on the flatlands / well below where your crags reach up to heaven.

Harvey, it should be noted, also wrote unflinching poems about the northern Troubles, not least 'The Lament of a Northern Ireland Child', whose final lines are an uncanny precursor of Michael Longley's 'Ceasefire':

> and I fear I may one day have to shake the hand that blew
> a crater in Johnnie's head the size of his mouth.

In her introduction to Harvey's *Collected Poems*, Moya Cannon speaks of his 'haiku-like attention and playfulness', further describing him as a 'Bashō-like figure'. It's fitting, then, that his final collection should be *Donegal Haiku*. He mostly adheres to a 5-7-5 syllable structure, and references the seasons in traditional haiku mode. There are plenty of nods to Japanese culture including Bashō, kimonos, cherry blossom – and Mount Fuji:

> Sleeping, I think of
> Errigal and Mount Fuji.
> The shape of my dreams.

Donegal Haiku is a beautifully structured sequence of haiku that follows a distinct arc – taking us through spring, summer, autumn, winter, and back to spring. There's a symphonic sweep to its repeated motifs and images. His landscapes teem with life. Birds abound – blackbirds, Brent geese, crows, cuckoos, petrels, owls, and swallows that 'never strike a false note'. The passing of time is a central concern of Harvey's, and this book is undoubtedly the work of a man considering cycles of time, and his own mortality.

These haiku are also Irish to the marrow. One can imagine the poet as an early Irish monk writing in the margins: 'Dreams of the Trappist: / snow falling on snow and clouds / colliding with clouds.' He writes of treeless Tory Island:

> What does Mary Anne
> from Tory want for her swing?
> The branch of a tree.

This Mary Anne is a familiar name in traditional song and poetry, and the above haiku is preceded by 'What did he taste when / he kissed the island girl's lips? / The sweetness of salt.' This is a play on the Ballycastle folk poet John Henry MacAuley's 'The Ould Lammas Fair':

> But the scene that haunts my memory is kissing Mary Ann
> Her pouting lips all sticky from eating Yellow Man

Donegal Haiku is a joy to read, its language defined by tender observation, and by what Harvey, in the poem 'Wittgenstein', once described as 'something mind inhabits, a bird in air'.

Mark Roper's *A Gather of Shadow* is divided into two sections – 'Keep-net', a series of nature poems; and 'A Gather of Shadow', a moving sequence of poems about his mother's death. There's a crepuscular atmosphere to this work. He takes us 'into the half-silence, the half-light, the in-between leavings of winter'. In the opening poem 'River at Night', he writes:

> … A shadow peels
> off a shadow,
> a night heron, perhaps, perhaps
> something else,
> a shape too vague to translate.

Roper is alert to momentary flashes of beauty, as when he describes a swallow in flight, 'the ink / of its wing / on the water'. He sees a poem as a 'keep-net', in which he attempts to contain that which is elusive, fleeting:

> O voice, this world
> you'd catch and keep
> shines and slips through
> each word you shape.

In 'A Gather of Shadow', Roper effectively sings his mother across the River Styx. As she lies dying, he tells us 'Each time the boatman comes / he finds no coins in your mouth'. These poems are delicately lyrical, marked by a skilled use of assonance and consonance:

> At dusk I'm drawn to the back lane
> to watch the new foal. It floats and folds
> around its mother, a giddiness, an armful
> of air barely touching the ground.

Roper's mother is connected throughout to water, swimming, rowing. In 'Last Breath', his mother breathes 'In and out, slow and steady / as the stroke of an oar'. She is anxious, fretful, 'a private soul', who 'hated the show of any feeling'. In 'Sea Fret', Roper locates her character within a terrifying incident in her youth when she nearly drowned after being lost in a sea fog or 'fret':

> You're back inside that fret again,
> this time no shore can be found
> and you're saying *I'm so sorry.*
> *I'm so sorry to let you all down.*

A Gather of Shadow is an utterly graceful collection, and there's a beautiful pull to Roper's fusion of the plaintive and the plain, which takes us through the process and ritual of a death, a wake, and a funeral. Finally, these poems are marked by a tenderness that often takes the breath away, as in 'Cold':

> ... allow

> your hands to relax
> and receive the sprigs

> of rosemary, beech
> and winter jasmine

> we place on them.

Doireann Ní Ghríofa

ASCENSOR

A funicular, this heart of mine – little more
than a clapboard cabinet on a cord,
drawn by string and whim. Like its sisters,
it see-saws up and down the slopes of Valparaiso.
In this land of cobbled alleys and painted streets,
it grinds a path from ocean to hilltop houses.
Inside, graffiti marks the small, scarred room
where teenagers with penknives once gouged
LOVE. The narrow door opens
and lets more passengers on – children, grandchildren.
The rope that bears such weight grows weak with age,
but every day, it lifts people up the hills and down again.

Katrina Naomi

THE IDEA OF A PLACE

Any woman might dissolve in this haze
as the bay's sleepy mouth regurgitates
its fill of fish at morning,
and the sun rims its orange into the hills.

She is fulmar-high, where a cloud hovers.
A shoal of curlew flit and flee,
the ocean grows momentarily dark –
a patch like danger a few leagues out.

A woman might lose herself up here,
do nothing but gaze amid the wood pigeons'
woo-woo wuh-woo, as life goes on
behind the town, beyond the church

with its fortifications keeping her kind out.
The light shifts, glares on the waves' skin.
She does her duty, keeps looking
down. The sun smarts. The sea knows

as much of her as this salty town.
She will not be believed, even as she lives
in the gap between other people's existence,
in the dusk of her own quiet company,

where soon she'll burrow deep into the hills
before they come and set them alight.

Philip Coleman

'TO BE COURAGEOUS & KIND': JOHN BERRYMAN AT 100

At a reading in the Andersen Library at the University of Minnesota in October 2014 to celebrate the centenary of John Berryman's birth – in a building that houses the poet's archive and personal library, less than a hundred yards away from where he took his life in January 1972 – the poet Henri Cole read selections from the poet's work that seemed to be chosen in honour of members of the Berryman family who had gathered for the occasion. Without drawing attention to her presence in the audience, Cole read Dream Song 171, in which Berryman praises the 'excellence' ('in every thing') of his third wife Kate Donahue. Cole chose texts in which Berryman's love for his family is expressed clearly but he handled the occasion with remarkable sensitivity. This was especially the case when, towards the end, he read the following excerpt from a letter Berryman wrote to his son Paul, then only four years old, in 1960:

> Dear Poukie, ...
>
> I miss you. I miss you every day, and I have done ever since I saw you last. I have long dreams (one last night) about you. [...] We look at the pictures of you so far off ...
>
> Now, you must remember what I say:
>
> 1) It is not possible for me to see you, much, if ever again. But you are to know that I love you. I will come as soon as I can. There is more to say about this.
>
> 2) You must be a *good boy* – obeying your very good mother – heading to some end *outside yourself* (far later, your mother will be able to explain this) – and with respect for your father, who has not been the most useless man in the present American world.
>
> 3) Then kick it all aside, – except for your veneration for your mother, – and do what *seems necessary* and consonant with your gifts, training, & allegiance.
>
> 4) *Strong fathers crush sons.* You are spared this, I think. (I am not able to form any conception of how my work will be regarded.) Go on.
>
> Yours, and w. love,
> John Berryman

As John Haffenden explains in *The Life of John Berryman* (1982), it is not known whether Berryman ever sent this letter to his son, but even if he did, what would a child make of such declarations and instructions? What matters, however, is that Paul Berryman ('Poukie') was also present on the occasion of the centenary reading in Minnesota, and he expressed warm gratitude to Henri Cole for reading this letter to him.

It is fair to say that everyone else who was there on the twenty-fifth of October this year also felt grateful to Henri Cole for having the courage to address members of the Berryman family in the way he did. In a way, his reading amounted to a public expression of gratitude to Berryman's widow and children (Paul, Martha, and Sarah) for supporting the work that many poets, scholars, students and fans of Berryman have done on him over the years since his death. The most intensely private messages and meanings of Berryman's work can only be truly understood by those to whom they were first addressed. For the rest of us who are not members of the Berryman family, we can appreciate from a respectful distance the deep care and love that underscored Berryman's familial commitments by reading those works, and Henri Cole demonstrated this in his reading. In a late poem called 'Message', published in *Love & Fame* (1970), Berryman wrote: 'The thing meanwhile, I suppose, is to be courageous & kind.' Cole's reading brought out the courage and kindness of Berryman the man, but it also reminded members of the audience of their responsibility to be 'courageous & kind' in their engagements with a poet – and his family – who have often been represented in terms that do not add up when one takes the evidence of the published and unpublished works on board. No one can know the pain that John Berryman's family suffered when the poet took his own life in 1972, and yet for many years critics and readers have assumed that it is their right to explain it by looking for clues in his work. Maybe this is inevitable, given the desperate desire many people have to know why someone would take his or her own life, but out of respect for the poet's family, and in recognition of the poet's living gifts – which survive him in the lasting legacy of his work – the focus on the tragedy of Berryman's death that has overshadowed his greatest achievements needs to be addressed. As he wrote to his son in 1960, he was *not* 'the most useless man in the present American world' of his time. Moreover, he sought at all stages in his career to direct his work towards 'some end *outside*' himself, beyond the very real pain and heartache endured at different times by his private self.

A brief consideration of Berryman's career as a scholar and academic demonstrates his commitment to the public work he did as an educator over several decades, from the 1940s right up to the week before he died in 1972. At the Minnesota conference to celebrate his centenary several former students, many of them now in their seventies and eighties, turned up to speak formally and informally of Berryman's brilliance in the classroom, while many others who knew him spoke of his loyalty as a friend and colleague. Referring to Berryman's poem 'To a Woman' (also from *Love & Fame*) the Minnesota-based author Judith Healey referred to the poet as a one of the first male feminists she knew, while other ex-students such as Charles Turchick (one of the so-called 'Minnesota 8' memorialised in a poem published in the first edition of *Love & Fame*) spoke of Berryman's support for students who were protesting against the Vietnam War throughout the 1960s. These are aspects of the Berryman story that are not generally known, and they have been elided over the last few decades by readings of the poet that insist on what may be termed the narrow confessionalism of his work – its introspective obsession with personal concerns. For critics who read Berryman – and other poets including Sylvia Plath, Anne Sexton, and Robert Lowell – in this way, Berryman's work is always looking inwards; it has nothing useful to say to the public world of his or our own time. That view is changing, however, and this year's centenary celebrations in Minnesota and Dublin have shown that more and more readers and scholars are turning to Berryman's work for reasons that have nothing at all to do with the tragic vicissitudes of the poet's private life.

Henri Cole begins his introduction to a re-issue of Berryman's *77 Dream Songs*, published by Farrar, Straus and Giroux this year, by stating that: 'There is no poet who sounds like John Berryman in his *77 Dream Songs*.' April Bernard, who has provided an introduction to a re-issue of *Berryman's Sonnets*, also published this year, describes how she returned to Berryman 'astonished and amazed' by his work. Nick Cave, in a note published on the back of a re-issue of *The Dream Songs*, says:

> The Dream Songs have given me more pleasure than any other poems I have ever read. They have been an integral part of my world since I discovered them twenty years ago. Berryman is the poet that just keeps on giving. The more you read, the more you get. Each poem trembles with a terrible, furious beauty that lies somewhere beneath the surface of his often perplexing words. Be patient and it will rise, magnificent, to the surface.

Cave's insistence that 'Berryman is the poet that just keeps on giving' is an affirmation of the generosity of Berryman's poetic vision and the way that his work rewards patient, open, and unprejudiced re-reading. Unimpeded by the dismissals of critics such as Robert Phillips in the 1970s, who condemned Berryman for what he termed the poet's 'literary offenses' in his later work, or Marjorie Perloff, who dismissed Berryman (and Robert Lowell) as a disengaged *poète maudit* in the 1980s, contemporary artists are responding to Berryman in ways that express more creative goodwill than all of the critical appraisals that have been written about the poet over the last four decades taken together. From the many contemporary poets who contributed to *Berryman's Fate: A Centenary Celebration in Verse*, also published this year by Arlen House, to works such as visual artist and sculptor Siah Armajani's 'Tomb for John Berryman', which was exhibited in New York this year, artists from various disciplinary backgrounds and contexts, from Ireland and the United Kingdom to South Africa, are beginning to recognise the same magnificence that Nick Cave perceives beneath the surface of Berryman's work.

Irish readers and poets seem to be particularly drawn to Berryman, possibly because of his close engagements with W B Yeats, which inspired the young American poet's first visit to Dublin in 1937. In the 1966-67 academic year Berryman returned to Dublin, with his wife Kate and their young daughter Martha, and the family lived at 55 Lansdowne Park in Ballsbridge. As a result, the later books of *The Dream Songs*, which were largely written during that year, are full of references to Yeats and Dublin, but other writers (such as Austin Clarke and Patrick Kavanagh) and places (including Cobh, Kilkenny, and Clonmacnoise) are also referenced throughout Berryman's great long poem. The late Dennis O'Driscoll was a devotee of Berryman – he had two photographs of the American poet over his desk – and the last book he published before he passed away in 2012, *Dear Life*, contains a reference to Berryman in a poem that takes the form of a Dream Song in its title sequence. Many other contemporary Irish poets, from John Montague – who knew Berryman well at various times in his life – to Paula Meehan, have celebrated the poet in verse this year, and in many ways their acknowledgements and reflections constitute a remarkable declaration of creative generosity towards a poet who has been badly served by his critics for several decades. On the basis of the papers that were presented this year at two conferences dedicated to Berryman's work in Dublin and Minneapolis, however, the critical situation with regard to Berryman is changing. Twenty-five papers, by scholars from around the world, given over a period of five days together with settings of the poet's work to music by students and performers from Trinity College, Dublin and Queen's University, Belfast, showed that a new generation of readers is emerging for whom Berryman's work rewards the most exacting and exciting forms of critical and creative engagement. 2014 has been a good year for Berryman and for Berryman Studies, but it has also been a year when artists of many different kinds – poets, painters, sculptors, musicians – have returned to him with a renewed sense of his work as a source of positive sustenance and enablement.

In his afterword to the *Berryman's Fate* anthology, Maurice Riordan asks if any other poet from his generation could have inspired such a positive response as Berryman did in his centenary year. It is impossible to tell, of course, and many of those poets most frequently associated with Berryman, including Lowell and Plath, are just as likely to become role models or sources of inspiration to people who write. In an interview filmed towards the end of the poet's life by the legendary

Minnesotan documentary-maker Al Milgrom, John Berryman said that he wanted to be remembered as someone who worked hard – that was all. No matter where one dips into Berryman's large body of work – early or late, in verse or in prose – one appreciates that this was a writer for whom the activity of writing required all of his attention, all of his intellectual and emotional resources, all of the time. In one of the most well-known Dream Songs (14) his speaker declares, self-mockingly, that he has 'no inner resources':

> Peoples bore me
> literature bores me, especially great literature,
> Henry bores me, with his plights & gripes
> as bad as achilles ...

The grammatical and syntactical oddity of these lines – 'Peoples' and 'achilles' are deliberate – points to a strategic playfulness in language that is present to every line Berryman ever wrote. 'I perfect my metres / until no mosquito can get through', he writes in Dream Song 297 – in which the Liffey also gets a mention – but in his approach to diction and form Berryman is a twentieth-century poetic master craftsman whose closest peers, in the art of poetry, are Gerard Manley Hopkins and Dylan Thomas, figures whose work he also knew and passionately adored.

In an essay on Thomas – whose centenary is also celebrated in 2014 – first published in 1940, Berryman said that the Welsh poet had 'extended the language and to a lesser degree the methods of lyric poetry'. The point may also be made in relation to Berryman's own work, because in *Homage to Mistress Bradstreet* and *The Dream Songs* in particular Berryman not only showed how language could be used in new ways but he also opened up new possibilities for lyric form in modern poetry. Berryman's work, then, extends the language and the methods of lyric poetry, but the responses that his life and example have inspired this year also represent profoundly important and positive advances in contemporary criticism and creative practice. In his introduction to a selection of Berryman's poems made for Faber and Faber's 'Poet to Poet' series in 2004, Michael Hofmann compared Berryman's presence in US American poetry to 'a sort of one-off comet that approached that cosy solar system, lit it up for a while, and then exited'. A decade after that assessment was made, Berryman's presence in late twentieth- and early twenty-first-century literary culture, on both sides of the Atlantic, is no longer in any doubt. Far from being a comet, he is a permanent fixture in the literary firmament, a presence whose influence across the arts is only beginning to become fully apparent.

Notes on Contributors

Asa Boxer's poetry has garnered several prizes and is included in various anthologies around the world. His books are *The Mechanical Bird* (Signal Editions, 2007), *Skullduggery* (Signal Editions, 2011) and *Friar Biard's Primer to the New World* (Frog Hollow Press, 2013). Boxer is also a founder and manager of the Montreal International Poetry Prize.

Daragh Breen was born in Cork. His work has been published widely in Irish literary journals, including *Poetry Ireland Review*, *The Stinging Fly*, *Cyphers*, *The SHOp*, and *Cork Literary Review*. He has read at the Cork Spring Poetry Festival and for Poetry Ireland's 'Introductions' series.

Martin Burke, from Ireland, currently lives in Flanders. He has published a number of books with small presses in Ireland, the UK, the USA, and Belgium.

Matthew Campbell is Professor of Modern Literature at the University of York. He is the editor of *The Cambridge Companion to Contemporary Irish Poetry* (Cambridge University Press, 2003) and the author of *Irish Poetry under the Union* (Cambridge University Press, 2013).

Liam Carson is Director of the IMRAM Irish Language Literature Festival. He is the author of *Call Mother A Lonely Field* (Hag's Head Press, 2010).

Philip Coleman is a lecturer in the School of English, Trinity College, Dublin, where he directs the M.Phil. in Literatures of the Americas programme. He is the author of *John Berryman's Public Vision: Re-locating 'the Scene of Disorder'* (UCD Press, 2014) and he edited *Berryman's Fate: A Centenary Celebration in Verse* (Arlen House, 2014). He also co-edited '*After thirty Falls': New Essays on John Berryman* (2007) and *Reading Pearse Hutchinson: from Findrum to Fisterra* (2011).

Joey Connolly lives in London and edits *Kaffeeklatsch*, a journal of poetry and criticism. He received an Eric Gregory award in 2012 and his first collection of poems is forthcoming from Carcanet Press in 2016.

Belinda Cooke was born in Reading of Irish parents. She completed her Ph.D. on Robert Lowell's interest in Osip Mandelstam in 1993. Her poetry, translations, reviews, and articles have been published widely. She has published three books to date: *Resting Place* (Flarestack Poetry, 2008); *Paths of the Beggar Woman: Selected Poems of Marina Tsvetaeva*, (Worple Press, 2008); and (in collaboration with Richard McKane) *Flags,* by Boris Poplavsky (Shearsman Books, 2009).

Ailbhe Darcy is a doctoral candidate at the University of Notre Dame, Indiana, writing on contemporary Irish poetry and secularisation. Her article 'Dorothy Molloy's Gurlesque Poetics' appears in *Contemporary Women's Writing*. Her collection of poetry, *Imaginary Menagerie* (2011), is available from Bloodaxe Books.

Tom Duddy was born in Shrule, Co Mayo in 1950, and died in Galway in 2012. His debut collection *The Hiding Place* (Arlen House, 2011) was short-listed for the Seamus Heaney Centre Poetry Prize and the Aldeburgh First Collection Prize. A posthumous collection, *The Years*, was published this year by HappenStance Press.

Gavan Duffy lives and works in Dublin. He is a member of Platform One Writers Group based in the Rua Red Centre in Tallaght. He has previously published in various journals including *Crannóg*, *Stony Thursday*, *South Bank Poetry Journal*, *Poetry Porch*, and *Boyne Berries*.

John Fitzgerald currently lives and works in Cork where he is Librarian of University College, Cork. He has been commended in a number of recent poetry competitions, and in September he received the 2014 Patrick Kavanagh Poetry Award.

Andrew Fitzsimons lives in Tokyo. He is the author of *The Sea of Disappointment: Thomas Kinsella's Pursuit of the Real* (UCD Press, 2008) and he edited *Thomas Kinsella: Prose Occasions 1951-2001* (Carcanet Press, 2009). His two poetry collections are *What the Sky Arranges: Poems made from the Tsurezuregusa of Kenkō* (2014) and *A Fire in the Head* (2014), both from Isobar Press. He was shortlisted for the Montreal International Poetry Prize in 2013.

Daisy Fried is the author of three books of poems, most recently *Women's Poetry: Poems and Advice* (University of Pittsburgh Press, 2014). She is a member of the faculty of the Warren Wilson College MFA programme for Writers.

Peggie Gallagher lives in Sligo. Her work has appeared in literary journals in Ireland, England and North America. She was shortlisted for the Strokestown International and Gregory O'Donoghue poetry awards, and won the Listowel Poetry Collection prize in 2012. Her first collection, *Tilth*, is published by Arlen House.

Eamon Grennan taught for many years at Vassar College, New York. His most recent collections are *Out of Sight: New and Selected Poems* (Graywolf, 2010) and *But the Body* (The Gallery Press, 2012). He has translated the poems of Leopardi and co-translated (with Rachel Kitzinger) *Oedipus at Colonus* (Oxford University Press, 2004). He lives in Poughkeepsie and in Connemara.

Olimpia Iacob is Associate Professor in Modern Languages at 'Vasile Goldiş', West University of Arad, Romania. Her book-length translations include prose and poetry by Cassian Maria Spiridon, Gabriel Stănescu, Gheorghe Grigurcu, Petre Got, Mircea Petean, Magdalena Dorina Suciu and George Vulturescu.

Jason Irwin (www.jasonirwin.blogspot.com), from Pittsburgh, is the author of *Watering the Dead* (Pavement Saw Press, 2008), and the chapbooks *Where You Are* (Night Ballet Press, 2014) and *Some Days It's A Love Story* (Slipstream Press, 2005). He is a former winner of the Transcontinental Poetry Award.

Scott Jamison is a poet and musician living in Belfast. His poetry has been published in *The Rialto*, *The Literateur* and *The Open Ear*. He is currently completing a Ph.D. at Queen's University, writing a poetic biography of the Fenian rebel John Boyle O'Reilly.

Nick Laird, from Co Tyrone, worked for several years in London and Warsaw as a litigator, and now teaches in New York. He has published two novels, *Utterly Monkey* and *Glover's Mistake*, and three collections of poetry, *To A Fault*, *On Purpose* and *Go Giants*. His awards include the Rooney Prize for Irish Literature, the Geoffrey Faber Memorial Prize, a Somerset Maugham award and the Ireland Chair of Poetry Bursary.

John MacKenna is the author of seventeen books – most recently, a reissue of his novel *Clare* and his new novel *Joseph*, both published by New Island Books in 2014. His next collection of poems is due from Doire Press in 2015.

Iggy McGovern is Fellow Emeritus in Physics at Trinity College, Dublin. His most recent publication is *A Mystic Dream of 4* (Quaternia Press, 2013).

Belinda McKeon is the author of two novels, the second of which, *Tender*, will be published by Picador in April. She lives in New York and teaches at Rutgers University.

John McKernan taught for 41 years at Marshall University. He lives – mostly – in West Virginia where he edits ABZ Press. His most recent book is a selected poems, *Resurrection of the Dust*. He has published poems in *The Atlantic Monthly, The Paris Review, The New Yorker, Virginia Quarterly Review, The Journal, Antioch Review, Guernica, Field*, and elsewhere.

Martin Malone won the 2011 Straid Poetry Award and the 2012 Mirehouse Prize. His first full collection, *The Waiting Hillside,* is published by Templar Poetry. Currently studying for a Ph.D. in poetry at Sheffield University, he edits *The Interpreter's House* poetry journal.

Christopher Mulrooney is the author of *symphony* (The Moon Publishing, 2014), *flotilla* (Ood Press, 2014), *viceroy* (Kind of a Hurricane Press, 2014), and *Grimaldi* (Fowlpox Press, 2014).

Katrina Naomi's pamphlet *Hooligans,* inspired by the Suffragettes, will be published by Rack Press in February 2015. Her poetry has appeared in the *Times Literary Supplement, The Poetry Review* and *Poetry London*. She is completing a Ph.D. in Creative Writing at Goldsmiths College, with a focus on violence in poetry. She lives in Cornwall (**www.katrinanaomi.co.uk**).

Doireann Ní Ghríofa is a bilingual poet (**www.doireannnighriofa.com**). Among her awards are the Ireland Chair of Poetry Bursary 2014-2015 and the Wigtown Award for Gaelic Poetry in translation. Her work in Irish is published by Coiscéim, and a first collection of poems in English is forth-coming in 2015 from Dedalus Press.

Mary Noonan's poems have appeared in *Cyphers, The Dark Horse, The North, The Poetry Review, Poetry London, The Stinging Fly*, and *The Threepenny Review*. She won the Listowel Poetry Collection Prize in 2010. Her first collection – *The Fado House* (Dedalus Press, 2012) – was shortlisted for the Seamus Heaney Centre Poetry Prize and the Strong/Shine Award.

Proinsias Ó Drisceoil is the author of many essays on the Gaelic literature of Ireland and Scotland. He is the author of *Ar Scaradh Gabhail: An Fhéiniúlacht in Cín Lae Amhlaoibh Uí Shúilleabháin* (Cork University Press, 2000) and *Seán Ó Dálaigh: Éigse agus Iomarbhá* (Cork University Press, 2007). He is a contributor to the *Oxford Dictionary of National Biography* and other works of reference.

Seosamh Ó Murchú, from Wexford, was editor of the magazine *Comhar*, and co-editor of the literary journal *Oghma*. He was among the prize-winners at the Strokestown Festival of Poetry in 2012. He is currently Senior Editor with An Gúm. *Rugadh Seosamh Ó Murchú i Loch Garman. Bhí sé ina eagarthóir ar* Comhar *agus ina chomheagarthóir ar an irisleabhar critice* Oghma. *Bhí sé i measc na nduaiseoirí ag Féile Filíochta Idirnáisiúnta Bhéal na mBuillí in 2012. Ina Eagarthóir Sinsearach sa Ghúm faoi láthair.*

Michelle O'Sullivan's first collection *The Blue End of Stars* was published by The Gallery Press in 2012, won the Strong/Shine Award for best first collection, and was shortlisted for the Michael Murphy Memorial Prize. She lives in Co Mayo.

James Conor Patterson is a student on the MA course in Creative Writing at Queen's University, Belfast. His work has appeared in a number of publications, including *Cyphers*, *Wordlegs* and *Southword*. In 2013 he won the iYeats Emerging Talent Award for poetry. He lives in his hometown of Newry, Co Down.

Justin Quinn lives in the Czech Republic. His most recent collection of poems is *Close Quarters* (The Gallery Press, 2011).

Padraig Regan, from Belfast, is currently studying at the Seamus Heaney Centre for Poetry. His recent work looks at the paintings of the Dutch Golden Age. His poems have recently appeared in *Abridged* and at **www.lifeboatbelfast.co.uk**

Sarah Sala earned her MFA in Poetry from New York University, and currently teaches College Writing in New Jersey. Her honours and awards include an Academy of American Poets Prize, the Marjorie Rapport Award for poetry and an Avery Hopwood Award for nonfiction. A selection of her poetry was chosen for publication in *The Dory Reader* Chapbook Series (Small Anchor Press, 2011).

Stephen Sexton lives in Belfast where he is a student at the Seamus Heaney Centre for Poetry. His poems have appeared in *Abridged, Ulster Tatler* and as part of *The Lifeboat* series of readings. He was the inaugural winner of the FSNI National Poetry Competition.

Peter Sirr – see page 90.

Adam J Sorkin is a translator of contemporary Romanian literature. Sorkin's translation (with Lidia Vianu) of Marin Sorescu's *The Bridge* (Bloodaxe Books, 2004) won the 2005 Poetry Society Corneliu M Popescu Prize for European Poetry Translation, and their version of *lines poems poetry* by Mircea Ivănescu was shortlisted in 2011.

Matthew Sweeney's most recent collection is *Horse Music* (Bloodaxe Books, 2013). Two small publications appeared in 2014: *The Gomera Notebook* (Shoestring Press) and *Twentyone Men and a Ghost* (The Poetry Business). A new collection, *Inquisition Lane*, is forthcoming from Bloodaxe Books in 2015. He is co-author, with John Hartley Williams, of the satirical thriller *Death Comes for the Poets* (The Muswell Press, 2013).

George Vulturescu has published more than a dozen poetry collections, among them *The North and Beyond the North* (2001), *Monograms on the Stones of the North* (2005), *Other Poems from the North* (2007), *The Blind Man from the North* (2009), and *Gold and Ivy* (2011 – in which 'The Angel at the Window' first appeared).

Adam White is from Youghal in east Cork. After many years working as a carpenter/joiner, he developed an interest in teaching English. His first collection of poetry, *Accurate Measurements*, was published by Doire Press in 2013, and was shortlisted for the Forward prize for best first collection. He now lives in Normandy.

Annie Elizabeth Wiles is from New Haven, CT, and has lived in Dublin for a year as a student on the M.Phil. in Creative Writing course at Trinity College, Dublin. She was co-editor of an online anthology produced by her class this spring, and has had work published in *The Bohemyth*. She performs her songs and poems at open mic nights, and is currently working on her first novel.

Robert Wrigley has published ten books of poetry, most recently *Anatomy of Melancholy and Other Poems* (Penguin, 2013) in the US; and *The Church of Omnivorous Light: Selected Poems* (Bloodaxe Books, 2013), in the UK. He is Distinguished University Professor at the University of Idaho.